The author, James Polk, has taught at Harvard, where he obtained his Ph.D. in English Literature, and at the University of Alberta.

**With the compliments of the Canada Council**

**Avec les hommages du Conseil des Arts du Canada**

# Wilderness Writers

canadian portraits

Ernest Thompson Seton
Charles G. D. Roberts
Grey Owl

# Wilderness Writers

James Polk

Clarke, Irwin & Company Limited
TORONTO / VANCOUVER

© 1972 by Clarke, Irwin & Company Limited

ISBN  0-7720-0565-6

No part of this publication may be reproduced
or transmitted in any form or by any means,
electronic or mechanical, including photocopy,
recording, or any information storage and
retrieval system now known or to be invented,
without permission in writing from the publisher,
except by a reviewer who wishes to quote brief
passages in connection with a review written for
inclusion in a magazine, newspaper or broadcast.

1 2 3 4 5 6    RF    77 76 75 74 73 72

## contents

The Animal Story in Canada / 2
Ernest Thompson Seton / 16
Sir Charles G. D. Roberts / 62
Grey Owl / 100

Wilderness Writers

# The animal story in Canada

*Eighteenth-century English "imaginings", based on Canadian accounts*

The first Canadian wilderness stories were Indian legends, and probably in no other culture has the relationship of man and beast seemed so harmonious. In the beginning of time, as it was told in many of these legends, Beaver, Muskrat, and Toad helped man — actually, woman, since she came first — by diving into universal waters to fetch up dry land. This they shaped into the earth, which rests on the shell of the Great Turtle.

Some animals climbed to heaven and became stars; others, like the god-like Raven and Coyote, roamed the world — changing shapes and getting in and out of jams. The Indian found religion, natural history, and entertainment in these great tales, and it was a long time before Canadian writers came up with anything half as good.

Of course, people have always told stories of animals and wilderness places. From our knowledge of his cave paintings, we can be sure that primitive man liked to hear hunting yarns after a hard day in the bush. Accounts of the wounded mammoth or the sabre-tooth that got away must have been hair-raising, when the huge beasts themselves snorted in the darkness beyond the campfire.

As civilization advanced, men seemed to prefer stories about strange, fantastic animals, and the bigger the better. Ancient Greeks delighted in flying horses and golden-fleeced rams, and many of their mythical beasts fill the night skies as constellations. Most of the world's religions include stories of marvellous animals too, such as the huge fish that swallows Jonah, and the seven-headed beast of the Book of Revelation.

For the Middle Ages, the wilderness was what God cast sinners out into, and animals were religious symbols. The pelican stood for Christ, because it supposedly fed its life-blood to its children; monkeys were creatures of the devil, because they seemed lacking in moral virtue. The natural histories of the time — called bestiaries, or beast-books — described unicorns, mermaids, and geese which grew on bushes, along with the real animals. Men's eyes, it seems, were too firmly fixed on Heaven above to give a careful look at the world below.

Nobody really seemed interested in the way actual animals lived. For centuries, the favourite type of animal story was the beast fable, which is about men, not beasts. In *Aesop's Fables,* or the stories of Reynard the Fox, animals are made to act and talk in ways that poke fun at human conduct. The beast fable is still with us today, in such works as George Orwell's *Animal Farm*, or the Pogo Possum cartoon strip.

Even in the great animal classics of the nineteenth century, there is usually more fantasy than fact. In Anna Sewell's *Black Beauty*, the horse understands perfectly what humans say and reflects upon social injustices like any well-educated Victorian maiden. The morally uplifting story about domestic pets has been written in Canada too, most successfully by Marshall Saunders, whose *Beautiful Joe* has been a longtime best seller.

Most of the British animal classics are clearly about disguised humans. Beatrix Potter's bunnies live in furnished burrows and wear little jackets, which might have disturbed Mr McGregor more than the lettuce thefts. In Rudyard Kipling's *Jungle Books*, a panther and a python lecture poor Mowgli on the Law of the jungle like crabby high-school principals. In *The Wind in the Willows*, small game animals find themselves stuck into the British class system, with Toad an aristocratic playboy, and Mole and Rat representing the solid, pipe-smoking middle classes. The weasels who take over Toad Hall get to be the wicked lower class, for Kenneth Grahame, the book's author, was no democrat.

These "animal" books are really the old beast fables all over again, and so are such American varieties as Uncle Remus's Br 'er Rabbit tales, Thornton Burgess's "Mother West Wind" series, Uncle Wiggily, and Donald Duck. Certainly there is no point in objecting to such delightful creations on the grounds that they aren't realistic, for we don't go to beast fables to find out how actual animals live. Another kind of story exists for this, and it was first introduced in the 1890's by two Canadians, Ernest Thompson Seton and Sir Charles G. D. Roberts.

Basing their work on scientific observation, these writers described the experience of real, wild animals in natural settings. The animals are given names and the incidents in their lives arranged in a dramatic way, but none wear clothes, drive cars, smoke pipes, or speak to humans. They do communicate with one another, but so do real animals. In his story, "Raggylug", Seton admits that he is translating from rabbit into English, but adds that he will repeat nothing real rabbits could not say.

The realistic animal story was something new in

literature: a readable combination of natural history and good storytelling. There had been attempts to perk up natural history with literary tricks before, but the results were not very lively. P. H. Gosse's *The Canadian Naturalist*, published in 1840, hit upon the idea of having a father and son talk about woodland facts in dialogue form:

> *Father.* — But here our well-known nimble little friend, the Red Squirrel *(Sciurus Hudsonius),* has crossed the road: he makes a very singular trail; his two fore feet being so short, make their marks close to each other, while the hind footsteps are quite wide apart, and now and then there is a little sweep from his brush of a tail.
>
> *Charles.* — Oh! the rogue! see, he has come direct from the barn; I warrant with some grains of wheat in his mouth, to be deposited in his hole beneath the gnarled root of some tree.
>
> *Father.* — The squirrel is particularly assiduous in his attentions to the barn as long as the wheat remains in it; nor does he altogether treat the oats with contempt.

Europeans may have wondered if such sparkling conversation was typical of life in Canada; if so, *The Canadian Naturalist* must have kept many prospective immigrants away. The pictures also gave a curious idea of the country, with MOOSE looking like a wart-hog on stilts and BARRED OWL appearing to be a loaf of diseased French bread stranded in a tree.

Seton and Roberts usually take the animal's point of view, and let the instincts of the animal and the laws of nature govern the action. In Seton's famous *Biography of a Grizzly*, for example, we learn to understand what it's like being a "rogue bear" as we follow its

*Moose and Barred Owl from The Canadian Naturalist*

development, from the cub's early days when it is orphaned and wounded, through its bad-tempered mature years, to its unhappy death.

Seton's bear thinks and has emotions, but always acts within its limits as an animal, its chief concerns being food, territory, and men with guns. Also, luck plays a large part in these realistic nature stories, as it does in a real animal's experience. Thus in Roberts' story, "The Last Barrier", the salmon struggling upstream can throw off a fisherman's hook, only to be swatted down at the next shallows by a black bear. Few of these stories have anything approaching a fairytale ending, since the life of a wild animal can be as cruel as it is exciting.

Despite their concern for realism, both writers were labelled fakes by critics who saw their work as little better than beast fables. Perhaps Seton does get swept away by the heroism of his animals and exaggerates, and Roberts, who unlike Seton was not a professional naturalist, may slip up on the odd factual detail. Perhaps animals really don't have the individual "personalities" Roberts and Seton give to them, although people with pets know that cats and dogs aren't all the same by any means. Since no man will ever know exactly how any animals think or feel, these stories will have to do, until the animals themselves can tell us what it's like to be them.

It is often said that Roberts originated the realistic animal story, although his earliest one, "Do Seek Their Meat From God", came out in 1892, and Seton had been writing nature sketches throughout the 1880's. Who got there first? Some say Seton is a scientist who happened to use fictional elements in his work and swear by Roberts; others see Roberts as an imitator of Seton's successes, with a fancy prose style to cover up his scientific weaknesses.

The answer to "Who put real animals into literature first?" probably depends on which writer the reader prefers. Seton and Roberts didn't bother to fight over it. Each admired the other's work, and both discovered new approaches to nature writing at about the same time. The thing that counts is their stories, which are enjoyable and informative.

It is not surprising that Canadians should be the first to develop this type of fiction, since Canada has always been a country of vast wilderness areas. The rugged Laurentian Shield covers nearly half the land mass and the realities of a harsh natural world are not far away from the nation's largest cities. Certainly a writer would think twice before turning an Ontario wolf and a Jasper Park grizzly into miniature persons with shoes, hats, and big vocabularies.

From the beginning, writing in Canada has centered upon the wilderness. Jesuit missionaries in the New France of the 1700's sent back descriptions of the wildlife, with water-colour sketches, to the French king. Europeans wanted to know what the place was like, and Canadians who could spare the time from clearing land and surviving winters to write, tried to satisfy foreign interest in the flora and fauna of the new land.

So explorers' diaries, natural histories, guidebooks, essays on hunting and fishing, and the like have been staples of Canadian writing for a long time. The titles of our early literary classics speak for themselves:

*From a French map of New France, about 1547*

Catharine Parr Traill's *The Backwoods of Canada*, for example, or Susannah Moodie's *Roughing It in the Bush*.

Canadian painting is also indebted to the land. The forest at dawn, the Rockies in the sunset, boats on the river at midday — these were the popular subjects for ordinary painters at the turn of the century, and still are. Paul Kane specialized in recording life on the western frontier, and his pictures of buffalo, hills and Indians are well known. Canada's most famous artists, the Group of Seven, set out to capture the brooding spirit of the north country in paint, and Emily Carr's studies of the west coast rain-forests seem to radiate the dynamic energy of nature.

The National Film Board is known all over the world for its short, documentary films showing landscapes and animals. In Canadian music, from pop songs to symphonies, composers strive to create sounds that will convey the spirit of the land. Interestingly enough, many of the Canadian pavilions at Expo 67 imitated the wilderness in their architecture, from the Prairie Provinces' tree-crowned hill of wood shingles to the rough outcropping of granite blocks which housed the Ontario exhibit.

It almost goes without saying that Canadian history and the wilderness have been closely connected, and the nation is identified by two wilderness symbols: the beaver and the maple leaf. The beaver doubtless does not feel patriotic about his vital role in Canadian development, but we owe a lot to the pelts of his forefathers, since trade in beaver fur opened up the country. In the early days, a beaver skin became the standard unit of barter, and the Hudson's Bay Company even issued a coin, the value of which equalled one beaver.

Today the image of the beaver is all around us, advertising everything from lumber to peanuts, and crouched on the back of the nickel. Canada (that is to say the two pre-Confederation provinces) was the first country in the world to put an animal on a postage stamp — a beaver, what else, posing thoughtfully on the nation's first issue, the three-penny red of 1851. However, that furry little Eskimo-created Ookpik is fast becoming another Canadian symbol, and tourists can take home almost any northern animal as a memento of their visit, from souvenir counters crowded with Eskimo soapstone carvings.

Whereas most nations put buildings or bigwigs on their paper money, Canada's has pictures of wilderness scenes from across the country — or at least it used to. The oil refineries on the new ten-dollar bill, replacing a view of Alberta's purple Rockies, may be a sign that the times are changing. Could it be that we are beginning to think of Canada in terms of industries, rather than in images from nature?

Probably not. In some ways, Canadians today seem more aware of their wilderness heritage than ever before. This is shown in the public concern over oil spills, mercury pollution, atomic weapons testing, and other technological threats to the environment. In most countries, the killing of harp seals or whales or wolves would never make the headlines; in Canada, it can become the subject of nationwide controversy.

This is because the wilderness to us is more than just an empty place out there; it is a part of every

*From a French water-colour sketch-book, about 1700*

*The "three-penny beaver"*

Canadian's idea of himself and his country. Even if he has never been out of downtown Montreal or suburban Vancouver, in his imagination he belongs to a place of thundering rivers, untrodden forests, spacious plains, sublime icefloes, and untamed animals. Without the land, what would we be?

Thus it is logical that Canadians should write sympathetically about the wild, and the tradition founded by Seton and Roberts has been carried on by such men as Roderick Haig-Brown and Fred Bodsworth. Grey Owl's work is in a slightly different vein, since he does not concentrate on animal biography or fiction (aside from the delightful *Sajo and her Beaver People*). But his books beautifully describe the outdoors and the activities of real animals, and perhaps his gift for writing about beavers has never been equalled.

The three writers whose life stories are told in this book have certain things in common. They were all ardent conservationists, long before "ecology" became a household word, and their work did much to alert readers to the need to protect our vanishing wildlife. They were also expert woodsmen, whose idea of heaven on earth was to slip away from civilization and take off into the Canadian interior with a packsack and a canoe.

All three were intrigued by the original men of the wilderness, the Indians. Seton devoted much of his life to preserving the ideals of the redman, both in his Woodcraft Movement and during the early years of the Boy Scouts, an organization he did much to bring into being. Roberts was made an honorary chief by the Sarcees, and Grey Owl, who was brought up in a small

English town, went one step further and became an Ojibway Indian.

But in their life histories, these three men were completely unlike one another. Grey Owl's incredible story, as an English boy who grew up to be a world-famous Indian author, lecturer, and champion of the Canadian beaver, is itself a modern legend of the wilderness. Seton's life was extraordinary in a different way: through sheer grit he managed to rise above poverty and ill health — being thwarted at every turn by a cantankerous father, but finally making a name for himself as an artist, writer, and naturalist. In strong contrast is Sir Charles G. D. Roberts' sunny childhood in New Brunswick, his rise to fame as "The Father of Canadian Poetry", his career as a college professor, and his later years in the sophisticated literary circles of New York, Toronto and London.

The Indian, the artist-naturalist and the professor — on the face of it, no three men could be more different. Yet the work of all three is deeply rooted in the Canadian wilderness, and to read Grey Owl's *Pilgrims of the Wild*, Seton's *Wild Animals I Have Known* or Roberts' *Kindred of the Wild,* is as refreshing as to breathe pine-scented northern air. Today these wilderness writers provide a handy escape from our world of freeways and high-rises, and through their realistic treatment of animals they have let readers all over the world share in a new discovery of man's natural heritage.

# Ernest Thompson Seton

*Seton (left) with Lord Baden-Powell*

It was late, but old Charlie Peel was telling his hunting stories, and Ernest Evan Thompson hoped the evening would never end.

"Then that bear stopped to plug up his wounds with grass, so I had the chance to reload and fire again." Charlie paused for dramatic effect. "It's a good thing he took time out for first aid or I wouldn't be here to tell you about it."

Most of the listeners around the Thompson fireside laughed, but Ernest commented thoughtfully: "So its animal instinct to stop the flow of blood was stronger than its instinct to attack. Or maybe the bear was just as confused as you were, Charlie."

"Well, leave it to you to see the bear's point of view," Charlie said, shaking his head with a smile. "Now let an old codger give you a tip. You'll never tell a good hunting yarn if you give too much sympathy to the animal, because ...."

"Ernest, are you still up?" Mr Thompson's voice cut through Charlie's sentence like a knife. "I thought I told you to get to bed an hour ago. We get up early around here."

There was an uneasy silence broken only by the crackling of the fire. The family knew there was trouble ahead when Mr Thompson spoke in such a cold, threatening tone.

"It wasn't quite an hour," Ernest said, but his voice trailed away at a nervous glance from his mother.

"I am used to being obeyed in my own house," Mr Thompson continued. "After all I have done for my sons, I expect them to pay attention to my wishes. Will someone please hand me the riding crop?"

Ernest looked over to the door where his father kept the short, braided whip with the stinging loop. The riding crop was supposed to be used on horses, but Mr Thompson applied it more often to Ernest and his nine brothers.

"I guess it's only natural that the son of an earl should be interested in hunting," Charlie Peel said, breaking the tension. "Doesn't your family have a big estate and deer park back in England, Mr Thompson?"

With relief Ernest saw his father's face relax into a smile, as it always did when anyone mentioned his aristocratic background.

"There's no estate any more. But I am indeed a Seton, the only male survivor of the Earl of Winton. My forefathers were heroes during the Jacobite uprising and fought bravely at the Battle of Culloden. They were branded as rebels, so the family had to change its name to Thompson when it moved to England."

"Well, how about that! An earl right here in Lindsay, Ontario!" Charlie Peel exclaimed, and Ernest wondered if anyone else noticed the twinkle in the old hunter's eyes. "You should claim your rightful title."

"I will some day." Mr Thompson looked proudly around at his boys. He had forgotten about the riding crop. "Never forget, my lads, that your name is Seton. I'll have the name changed legally some day, but, of course, I'm too busy with the farm to do it right now."

Even Charlie Peel could think of nothing to say to this. Mr Thompson always talked about being busy, but most of the actual work of the farm was left to his sons and the hired help.

"Hmmm. Well, I guess I'd better let you folks get your sleep," Charlie said tactfully, rising to leave.

"Ernest, you come on over tomorrow and I'll tell you some more bear stories — even if you always do end up taking the side of the bear."

Ernest went upstairs happily. Not only had he escaped a sore backside: tomorrow he could slip away to the Peels', where Charlie's seventeen children and their assorted pets lived in an atmosphere of genial fun sadly missing from his own home. Once in bed, he put himself to sleep trying to remember a time when his father had not been so stern and dissatisfied.

In England, Joseph Thompson had been a wealthy partner in a shipbuilding firm, but a series of business failures made him decide to emigrate to Canada in 1866. Ernest, born on August 14, 1860, remembered very little about England and not very much about the trip, except for the great rock of Quebec seen from the ship's bow and the fireflies glittering like sparks outside the train window as they travelled across the lonely miles of Ontario bushland. But he did remember how his father's temper had grown steadily worse as it became clear that starting a farm in Canada was not the easy way to fame and fortune.

Ernest, however, loved Lindsay, especially the rich variety of animal and bird life in the woods around the small settlement. There he saw his first deer and discovered a squirrel's nest and found an abandoned baby crow which he tried, unsuccessfully, to raise himself. His greatest pleasure was tramping through the countryside with his brothers and the Peel children, although he noticed that the other boys did not get as excited as he did about the natural wonders they encountered.

One day he watched breathlessly as a small black-

and-white bird sailed out of the trees and boldly attacked a group of crows flying past.

"What was that?" he asked.

"Oh that. That was a kingbird," said one of the boys without much interest.

"A kingbird!" Ernest was overwhelmed. He had seen pictures of the bird in books but had never dreamed of spotting the real thing so close to home. In his imagination Ernest made a hero of the pint-sized warrior which could so fearlessly put to flight creatures much larger than itself. Many years later as a respected author, he was to write in his autobiography that the sight of this bird was the beginning of all his work as a creator of animal stories.

In his four years at Lindsay, Ernest learned many other things that would prove valuable later in life. Southern Ontario was still considered the frontier in the 1860's, and the pioneers had to do everything for themselves or go without. At an early age Ernest was taught the right way to saw wood, tie knots, and use hickory saplings to make axes. He found out which plants were edible and which ones brought on stomachaches. Like all the Lindsay boys, he knew how to make his own baseballs and bats, and once, with the aid of his eldest brother, he even managed to build a small stone house.

Ernest was thriving on frontier life, but his father and the farm were not doing so well. In 1870, Mr Thompson sold the farm and moved his family to Toronto, where he found work as an accountant and a house in one of the poorer sections of town. For the ten-year-old Ernest it was definitely a change for the worse. At that time Toronto had only a population of some 56,000 people, but after Lindsay the city seemed like a crowded, dirty monster to him.

Unfortunately, he and his brothers found themselves attending one of the toughest schools in town. Many of their classmates carried knives, and a high percentage of the boys served at least one term in jail before they graduated. Their way of welcoming newcomers was to test them in a fight. The first months of school in Toronto were a nightmare for Ernest, who was small for his age and not used to hand-to-hand combat.

As a young child, an unlucky accident had left Ernest with badly crossed eyes. The condition improved as he got older, but still, when anybody called attention to it, his eyes would cross automatically. His new classmates were delighted to discover this weakness and scarcely a day went by when Ernest did not hear the familiar warcry: "Hey Squinty, cross your eyes!"

No coward, Ernest would call back something equally complimentary, and the fight would be on. With so much practice, he soon learned to match skill and agility against an opponent's greater strength, and by the end of the year was winning as many battles as he lost. But oh, how he wished they had never left Lindsay!

Homesick for the woods, Ernest spent much of his free time roaming through the glens and ravines on the outskirts of Toronto. In the 1870's, areas like Queen's Park, the Rosedale hills, and the Don Valley were still virgin wildernesses, and there Ernest could escape the miseries of school and home. Mr Thompson's temper had not grown any better in the city and he did not approve of his son's passion for the outdoors.

"No gentleman I have ever known loafed around the

country the way you do," observed Mr Thompson, reaching for the riding crop. "I don't see why you can't stay home with the rest of the boys and help your father, after all he has done for you. Bend over."

Since he was not officially permitted to go out into nature, Ernest decided to bring nature into the house. He had seen a small collection of stuffed birds in a hardware store at Lindsay, and with typical energy and ingenuity he set about raising money for a wildlife museum of his own. He engraved a wooden block which could be rubbed with chalk and which printed the word "FOOL" when pressed on the back of a person's jacket. These blocks were a great success at school at two cents apiece. He also started a school-wide newspaper and invented a marble game and a cage for trapping grasshoppers. He collected used dime novels, the ancestors of our modern comic books, and sold them back to news-stand agents for a penny.

Some of the money he earned went towards buying a widely-advertised book called "Doctor Ross's *Birds of Canada*", which Ernest hoped would solve all his problems in identifying the birds he saw on his secret rambles. The book was so unscientific that Ernest had to fill in the margins of its pages with careful drawings and explanations of his own. Much later he would realize that his first serious work as a naturalist began because Dr Ross had written such a bad book.

Interested in everything to do with the outdoors, Ernest was naturally attracted to the life of the Indian. He was an avid reader of James Fenimore Cooper's novels, and organized the neighbourhood children to perform a play he had written in which the Indians triumphed over the invading white men. He wanted to form his own Indian tribe too, but his new Toronto friends wanted to be robbers instead, so Ernest had to be content with the leadership of a Robin Hood band. He made up a secret language for his Merry Men and had them dig a large robbers' cave under the Thompson house.

One day while his mother was sewing, she dropped her workbasket and was startled to see all the spools and thimbles roll directly to the northwest corner of the room.

"There's something funny about this floor," she complained to Mr Thompson. "You'd better test it with your carpenter's level."

Ernest froze, listening to his father's sniffs and murmurs as he examined the corner.

"This is strange," said Mr Thompson. "The house seems to be sinking. I'll go outside and take a look."

He left, and after a few minutes a loud cry told Ernest that the secret hideout had been discovered. If only his friends had accepted the idea of the Indian tribe — but it was too late to think about that.

He got a solid thrashing over the cave incident, but in many respects his life in Toronto was slowly improving. In 1872, the Thompsons moved to a better part of town and Ernest could transfer to a less bloodthirsty school, where he promptly earned a scholarship to the Collegiate High School for students planning to enter University. He studied harder than ever now, for he knew his father would never finance a college education. A university scholarship seemed the only way to escape the oppressions at home, since Ernest didn't want to imitate his elder brothers, stuck in what he considered dreary, closed-in jobs as clerks and bookkeepers.

On Saturdays, however, Ernest forgot schoolwork and his father's temper and went exploring the country north of the city. One day, when he was fourteen years old, he came upon a beautiful, thickly wooded glen hidden in one of the ravines. There was a clear brook running through it, and only the chatter of birds and squirrels broke the hushed silence. Ernest felt he must be the first man ever to look upon this place, and he solemnly claimed it for his own.

With great care and labour he built a small cabin near the brook and for more than a year spent every Saturday there, trying to live up to his own ideal of Indian life. He made crude moccasins out of old sheep leather, daubed his face with clay and stuck a feather in his hair, and "White man heap no good" became his favourite phrase. Here in his private paradise he spent some of the happiest days he had ever known, collecting wildlife specimens and imitating all the customs of the red man.

He told no one about his secret, and the cabin was his retreat from all the problems of his "real" life in Toronto. Then one day, escaping to the glen after a particularly severe beating from his father, he noticed human footprints in the underbrush. His heart sank. Crawling silently through the thicket, he reached the brook and saw — in his cabin — three rough-looking tramps playing cards and drinking redeye. Ernest did not watch them for long. He crept away, feeling as if his whole world had collapsed around him. When he got the courage to return several weeks later, he found that the men had wrecked the cabin completely and polluted his brook with garbage and bottles.

It was a great shock. Ernest brooded over his loss for the rest of the school year and by summer was in such poor physical condition that the doctor ordered rest in the country. Luckily the old farm at Lindsay was now owned by Mr Blackwell, his father's former hired hand, and he offered to take Ernest in until his health improved.

Ernest soon found that Mr Blackwell's son, Sam, shared his own interest in nature and Indian life, and they took time off from chores to set up a bark wigwam together. In spite of their hard work, the structure was a flop: the smoke hole wouldn't draw, and a stiff wind finally blew the whole thing to shambles. But Mr Blackwell himself had become interested in the project.

"There's canvas in the barn you boys can use for your teepee," he told them. "And get old Caleb Clark to help with the building of it. He's a strange cuss, living out there in the woods by himself, but there ain't nothing he don't know about the Indians and their ways."

With Caleb's help the new teepee was a success, and the old man also gave Sam and Ernest tips on fire-making, shooting home-crafted bows and arrows, and interpreting animal tracks. Also, a pipe-smoking old lady nicknamed "The Lindsay Witch" showed them what herbs were good for medicines, dyes and foods, and they learned from her how to live off the land.

Mr Blackwell was as intrigued with the experiment as the boys were themselves, and one day suggested: "No sense in you two coming back and forth from the teepee to home every day. If you're going to be real Indians, you got to go all the way."

"You mean we can camp out in the teepee?" Sam asked.

"Don't see why not, as long as you can talk your brothers and sisters into doing the chores for you. Now mind, it won't do if you come running back at the first drop of rain, or turn up begging your mother for supplies. You'll do it Indian-style, or not at all. And if I hear that you are shooting songbirds, or messing up the countryside, or setting fire to the woods, I'll have your hides for it."

Ernest looked at this rough, illiterate farmer with something close to hero-worship in his heart. Here was a man who treated boys with respect, a father who took it for granted that his son's interest in woodcraft was a serious matter. He ruled his children with a firm hand, but he always listened to their side of the story and never strapped them without just cause. Ernest could not help comparing Mr Blackwell's no-nonsense attitudes with his own father's ideas of refinement and discipline. Needless to say, Mr Thompson did not come out very well in the comparison.

The summer was like a dream come true for Ernest, and he later wrote about it in the enduring classic, *Two Little Savages*.

>"What you got?" called Sam, as he saw Yan bending eagerly over something down by the pond.
>
>Yan did not answer, and so Sam went over and saw him studying out a mark in the mud. He was trying to draw it in his note-book.
>
>"What is it?" repeated Sam.
>
>"Don't know. Too stubby for a Muskrat, too much

claw for a Cat, too small for a Coon, too many toes for a Mink."

"I'll bet it's a Whangerdoodle."

Yan merely chuckled in answer to this.

"Don't you laugh," said the Woodpecker, solemnly. "You'd be more apt to cry if you seen one walk into the teepee blowing the whistle at the end of his tail. Then it'd be, 'Oh, Sam, where's the axe?' "

"Tell you what I do believe it is," said Yan, not noticing this terrifying description; "it's a Skunk."

That summer in Lindsay, Ernest became healthy as an ox, and he spent many hours roaming the woods to satisfy his curiosity about wildlife. He began to make sketches of the birds and beasts he observed and took notes on unusual aspects of animal behaviour to preserve them in his memory. Convinced that a naturalist's life was the only one for him, he resolved to win a scholarship in zoology at the University. Money had always impressed Mr Thompson, and he couldn't offer many objections if someone else was paying the bills.

After his months in this paradise, going back to Toronto and the Thompson household was like a descent into hell. Determined to escape through a scholarship, Ernest threw himself blindly into his schoolwork. He studied constantly, often skipping meals and staying up as late as he dared to perfect his assignments. This kind of life soon destroyed his health again, and one night, while preparing for the Christmas exams, he was suddenly overcome with a strange dizzy sensation. The room seemed to spin around him, and murmuring "I can't study, I can't study," he fell to the floor in a faint.

The doctor diagnosed the trouble as lung fever and

held out little hope for a recovery. Further schoolwork was out of the question, so Ernest spent most of that year being fed and cared for by his mother. Even Mr Thompson was moved by the seriousness of his son's condition and went so far as to buy him a rifle he had always wanted. Showered with all this unusual kindness and attention, Ernest improved rapidly and by the following summer he was able to go north to recuperate at the farm of an old Lindsay acquaintance near Fenelon Falls.

The vacation was almost fatal. The farmer became ill and had to be taken into town, and this left Ernest alone with his wife and daughters. Then the entire household came down with malaria, or "shakes fever" as it was called in those days. Ernest was no exception, and spent the long days wrapped in a blanket — alternately shivering with icy chills or parched by raging fever. There was no way to contact the outside world, and nobody was strong enough to do more than crawl down to the stream for water. Provisions were speedily exhausted. As the month of August dragged by, Ernest and the others lay inside the hot cabin like rag dolls, too feeble to move.

Then he began to have hallucinations: a blacksnake he had noticed in the woodpile seemed to be a ten-foot dragon-fanged monster. In his delirium he raved about the reptile, and expected that at any moment it would glide through a window and devour them all. Eventually a dangerous animal did get into the cabin, and it was no hallucination.

It happened after Ernest had boiled a chicken, and leaving half the carcass on the table, had dropped off to sleep. He woke up to find a full-grown lynx licking the last chicken scraps off the now-empty dish. Ernest groaned and the beast left at once through an opening in the cabin wall, while the invalid tried to convince himself it had been a nightmare. But there was the dish, definitely without its chicken. With weak, shaking hands he filed a point on an old-fashioned fishing spear, and wondered if he would have the strength to defend himself if he had to.

Several nights later, the lynx was back, lapping water from the bucket right by Ernest's bed. He let out a yell, calling to the women in the other room: "Jane! Kate! The lynx is here again!"

"Then may God help ye," came the hopeless response, "for we cannot!"

Somehow he lit a candle and made a quaking sort of lunge at the beast with his fish-spear. With ears flattened back and tail lashing, the lynx streaked under the bed. As Ernest tottered towards the pair of eyes gleaming in the shadows, he could hear the women wailing and praying in the next room. Summoning every ounce of energy he possessed, he plunged the spear beneath the bed. There was a screech as a claw swiped out at him; then he heard teeth gnawing at the spear-shaft and held on for dear life.

At last, the lynx wrenched away, breaking off the shaft with the point still buried in its chest. With a yowl of rage it slunk through the opening and vanished into the night, never to return. Ernest sank in a faint on the bed, all his energy utterly wasted.

One day in September the head of the family returned.

"Hello in there, anybody home?" came the chipper voice from outside the door. "Are you all dead in there?"

"Just about," croaked Ernest.

"Ye all are no better than skin and bones," the farmer exclaimed after a shocked investigation. "Why didn't ye let me know?"

At this, Ernest managed something between a laugh and a gasp of agony, and looked around for something to throw.

With doses of quinine, his mother's cooking, and a long rest at home, Ernest recovered from his "vacation". But as he got better, his father's temper seemed to get worse, and soon not a day went by without a pointed remark from Mr Thompson about sons who loafed around the house all day when they could be out supporting their aged parents.

"So Ernest, you're sixteen years old. What do you plan to do with your life?"

"I've already told you what I want to be. A naturalist."

"A naturalist?" Mr Thompson exploded. "What kind of profession is that for a gentleman, tramping around the woods like a hobo and staring at the birds? Where's the money in it? No, there's no future in becoming a naturalist, and I won't allow it."

"Well then, what will you allow?" Ernest said, trying to hold back his anger. "What do you want me to do?"

"Become an artist, my boy. Now there's a career with refinement! Don't think I haven't noticed your knack for drawing and painting, which, I may say, you inherited from me. I might have been a first-rate artist myself, if I had ever taken the time to be properly trained."

Since there seemed to be no hope of becoming a naturalist, Ernest accepted his father's decision. He did enjoy sketching wildlife, and if he couldn't study animals scientifically, he might as well paint their pictures. But he couldn't help smiling when he realized how many parents would have objected to an artist's career for their sons. Would he ever understand his father's way of reasoning?

He began as an apprentice for a popular Toronto painter who did portraits of fashionable people in society. Ernest did not learn very much from this man, who copied photographs projected directly onto the canvas and who used the same colours and backgrounds for all his pictures. Ernest received no salary, but he earned money at the boxing academy above the artist's studio, by painting over black eyes with flesh-tints. Realizing that he was not getting a very sound training in the fundamentals of art this way, he enrolled in night classes at the Ontario School of Art, and in 1879 won the gold medal as the most outstanding student.

"I have been awarded the highest honour at the best art school in Canada," he told his father. "If you really want me to be an artist, you must now send me to study in London."

Mr Thompson was reluctant, but he couldn't deny the logic of his son's argument. He agreed to support the boy in London for a year.

"It's only a loan, you understand," he added gruffly. "I'm not a rich man."

So, on June 12, 1879, Ernest watched the small lakeport of Toronto growing smaller as he stood on board the ship bound for Europe. He was sorry to leave his mother and the familiar Canadian countryside he loved so well, but it seemed that a new chapter in his life was beginning. He would be on his own at last.

In 1879, London was the largest and most powerful city in the world, and it is not surprising that the nineteen-year-old artist from Canada felt shy and awkward among his sophisticated fellow students. However, on his second attempt at the competitive entrance examinations, he was granted one of the two scholarships given annually by the Royal Academy School of Painting and Sculpture. It was an honour which carried with it many privileges, including free admission to the London Zoo, where Ernest could observe wild animals and exotic birds at close range.

It was a hard life Ernest led in London, for the simple reason that his father would not send him enough money. Ernest wrote long, prayerful letters saying he was starving to death, but the regular allowance he had been promised was never sent. During his two years in England, he received a total of approximately three hundred dollars from home, and it was not far from the truth when he complained of starvation. In an unheated room the ragged young student lived almost entirely on beans and porridge and a kind of "coffee" he had invented for himself out of bran and molasses.

Yet Ernest learned a great deal at the Academy and was fond of walking around the streets of the bustling metropolis. His scholarship included a Reader's Permit to the British Museum, although at that time the natural history collection was not open to students.

Finding this out, Ernest went straight to the Head Librarian and soon convinced him of his sincere desire to study the rare books and drawings so strictly guarded.

"I'd let you in if I could," sighed the Librarian. "But even I don't have the authority to do that."

"Who does?"

"Why, the trustees of the Museum."

"And who are they?"

"They include the Prince of Wales, the Archbishop of Canterbury, and the Prime Minister."

"I shall appeal to them," said Ernest, and the Librarian, smiling at the young man's audacity, bowed him out of the office.

That night, Ernest had second thoughts as he finished writing his letters to three of the most important men in England. It was not likely that they would pay attention to a plea from a poor art student who wanted to study books on nature. But there was no harm in asking, so he posted the letters. Three days later he received encouraging replies, and two weeks after that he was given a rare privilege: a Life Member's Ticket to the Museum. Now the Librarian gladly showed him the treasures of the natural history collection, and here Ernest first saw the books of Audubon, Wilson, Thoreau, Burroughs, and many other well-known naturalists. He spent much of his time reading and sketching in the Museum from then on, delighted with the wealth of knowledge spread before him. He felt he had come a long way from the days when he had so painstakingly pored over the inadequate pages of Doctor Ross's *Birds of Canada*.

In his second year in London, Ernest had learned

enough about animals and art to sell some wood engravings to publishers for small sums. But his cold room and meagre diet were steadily undermining his health. Perhaps his physical condition had something to do with the mysterious voices he began hearing in the summer of 1881. At first he could make nothing out of the mutterings, which seemed to come from nowhere, but then a single Voice began to predict the future course of his life in firm, but gentle tones. Ernest had assumed that he would stay in London and make his way as an illustrator of books, but the Voice had another message.

"A year from now you will be living on the Plains of western Canada. You will there regain your health.... Your future will be, not in Canada or London, but in New York, where, as an illustrator and writer, you will make your fortune."

Later Ernest was to call this mysterious Voice his "Buffalo Wind", summoning him to the open skies of the west and to his destiny. He was not particularly surprised when a letter from his mother arrived shortly thereafter, ordering him to come back to Canada for his health's sake. He had only enough money for passage on a cattle ship and the rough Atlantic crossing was another trial for his frail physique. For weeks, itching from lice and crowded by poor immigrants, he lay on a straw pallet in the dark, airless hold, as storms battered the ship.

Back in Toronto, not quite two and a half years after he had left, his mother's meals and his daily walks in the ravines worked their usual magic. However, the sour looks from Mr Thompson at the dinner table reminded him that he was still penniless and unemployed. One day his father called him into his study, took down a heavy accounts book and opened it at the letter "E".

"Ernest, now that you are twenty-one, you are a man. Everything I have done for you, you must now do for yourself, but I need hardly remind you how much you are indebted to me. You owe everything on earth, even life itself, to your father; reverent gratitude should be your only thought. It is impossible that you should ever discharge *this* debt, but there is yet another to which I must call your attention."

Mr Thompson pointed to the entries in his book. Every cent he had ever spent on Ernest was listed there, neatly dated, beginning with the doctor's fee for bringing his son into the world. The total amount was $537.50.

"Up to now I have charged no interest," said the old man, his voice trembling at the thought of his own generosity. "But hereafter I must add six per cent per year. Naturally I shall be glad to have you reduce the amount at the earliest opportunity."

Ernest sat thunderstruck. He opened his mouth, but the words seemed to be stuck in his throat. His father looked at him suspiciously and said: "Is there any question about my addition?"

"N-no," Ernest managed to blurt out.

"I'll be glad to furnish you with a full copy of the bill at no extra expense."

"No, thank you."

"Good, my son. Naturally you cannot remain as an inmate of this house much longer, but I trust that wherever your lot is cast, you will never forget the debt you owe your father, who is to you, on earth, the next to God."

Ernest left the room like a sleepwalker, and then rushed out of the house. He hiked for miles — paying no attention to where he was going and trying to make some sense out of what had happened. When he returned home, there was a bitter determination inside him to pay off the so-called debt as soon as possible, and to leave his father's house once and for all.

The next day Ernest got a job making bird drawings for Christmas cards and earned the princely sum of sixty dollars. He thought of giving it to his father, but then remembered his "Buffalo Wind" telling him that his true destiny would take him to the west. His brother Arthur had a homestead in Manitoba and had written that cattle and other stock were fetching high prices on the prairie. Ernest couldn't afford cattle, but he staked his earnings on some chickens and a railroad ticket, and on March 16, 1882, he left Toronto. It was his hope that this time he could gain complete independence for himself and eventually pay off the hateful debt.

At that time the Canadian Pacific Railway had not been completed, and it was a long, tedious journey, down to Chicago and then north through the Dakotas, to reach Winnipeg. To make matters worse, Ernest's train was halted by blizzards for days at a time and as food supplies ran low he subsisted on the raw eggs laid by his hens. But despite the rigours of the trip, Ernest was impressed by the snow drifting for miles around the train like a white, frozen sea and by the vastness of the pale-blue prairie skies.

As they neared Winnipeg, there was something

which thrilled him even more. In a glade he saw a pack of dogs holding an enormous solitary wolf at bay. Ernest realized that this must be the notorious Winnipeg Wolf, which preferred the city to the country, killed dogs instead of sheep, and always hunted alone. Before the train passed by, Ernest watched the pack of dogs attack and the magnificent beast drive them away with scornful ease. Ernest instinctively knew that this country with its immense open spaces and unusual animals was just the place for him.

He was right. A homesteader's life was rugged, but Ernest had never been afraid of hard work, and the excitement of settling a new frontier reminded him of the early days at Lindsay. Also, the prairie wildlife was a source of endless fascination, and he began to take a notebook on his walks, and to record the data which would be later transformed into respected works of natural history. By the end of his life the notebooks, crammed with sketches and measurements, filled fifty huge, leatherbound volumes, and when aspiring naturalists came to him for advice he would say: "The first rule is, keep a full and accurate notebook at all times. You can't do without it."

Ernest drew the shapes of hawks and ducks and discovered the eggs of several birds which had never been catalogued by scientists before. He also became absorbed in the weird "dance" of the grouse, or prairie chicken, and would often trek out before dawn to witness the performance.

The grouse would gather on a low mound, completely bare of vegetation. As the eastern sky began to brighten, the leader would lower his head, spread his wings, lift his tail, and run furiously over the ground. The others would then join in, the prairie throbbing like a drum under their pounding feet, a gibbering noise coming from the air sacs at their throats. After this wild, noisy hoedown, they would fall quiet, as if stunned by the outburst of energy. Then it would begin again.

Most people assumed this was some sort of mating ritual, but Ernest proved otherwise. He had fifteen baby grouse which had hatched under an ordinary barnyard hen. During a cold snap he brought the chicks inside and put them on the protective sheet of tin under his brother's pot-bellied stove. A ray of sunlight suddenly streamed in upon the birds, and one lowered its tiny head, raised its behind and hightailed it across the tin, and as it ran it made a high-pitched gargling sound. The others followed suit — performing to perfection the ballet of the older grouse, which they had never seen. Ernest found he could start the dance himself by tapping on the tin, and realized that the instinct to express their healthy joy in living was present in prairie chickens long before their sexual maturity.

Ernest had not been so happy since the early days at Lindsay. Like any westerner he soon learned to take in his stride the blizzards and low temperatures that seemed to announce the beginning of another Ice Age. By the end of the first winter, he was an expert in forecasting the weather from a glance at the sky and could read the stories told by animal tracks in the snow. As the Voice had predicted, his broken health was on the mend, and he felt there was nothing in the world that could mar his happiness now.

# SPECIAL ANNOUNCEMENT
## SEASON OF NINETEEN HUNDRED THREE AND FOUR

# ERNEST THOMPSON

 # SETON

### AND HIS
## Wild Animal Friends

MR. WILLIAM SMITH WILLIAMS takes great pleasure in announcing that he has completed arrangements for the exclusive management of MR. ERNEST THOMPSON SETON'S lectures for the coming season, and is now offering the public an extended opportunity of seeing and hearing the most noted naturalist and student of Wild Animal Life of the day.

During the last season Mr. Seton has traveled and lectured twenty-six weeks, averaging ten lectures a week; in all, two hundred and sixty lectures, covering about twenty-six thousand miles travel in thirty-two states, including Utah, California, Oregon, Washington, British Columbia, Manitoba and Ontario. During that time he has addressed over 300,000 children and 200,000 grown-ups. Everywhere crowded houses welcome him. Invariably the matinee lectures have the largest attendance, mostly children. The whole human family is his public, because every human being loves wild animals; the rich and the poor, the learned and the unlearned, are alike interested and enthusiastic auditors.

All of Mr. Seton's writings and drawings descriptive of the personality of wild animals are enhanced many fold by his inimitable description of them from his own lips. It is seldom that an author-artist is gifted with the ability to entertain upon the lecture platform, but Mr. Ernest Thompson Seton is as clever with his voice as with his pen and pencil.

IN ODD CATLIKE POSITIONS

## LECTURES FOR SEASON 1903-1904

THE PERSONALITY OF WILD ANIMALS
    WILD ANIMALS I HAVE KNOWN
        WILD ANIMALS AT HOME
ANIMAL HEROES
      NEW ADVENTURES OF ANIMAL FRIENDS
        THE INDIAN AS I KNOW HIM (New)

*Paintings and drawings by E. T. Set...*

"Leaping Wolf"

From "The Wolves' Triumph"

One May morning he returned to the cabin with his brothers Arthur and Charlie, to find Mr and Mrs Thompson and four other members of the family waiting for them.

"I have decided to give up my job in Toronto," Ernest's father said. "I'm going to move in here with you. It's high time my sons started supporting me, in return for all I have done for them."

Ernest stared at his father in disbelief. Was there no escape? It was all he could do to be polite to his parents and welcome them to the west.

But the west did not suit Mr Thompson and he left for Toronto after a few weeks — complaining about the raw spring weather on the prairies and the poor sort of accommodation his sons had provided.

In 1883 Ernest went to Chicago to consult a celebrated doctor about his health. After the visit and a cure, he returned to the homestead at Carberry, Manitoba, and the period began which he was to call "my golden years". In peak physical condition for the first time in his life, he could stride for miles over the plains — searching out new facts for his notebooks. He spent so much time out of doors in a certain group of sandhills that the neighbours began calling the area "Seton's Kingdom".

It was legally "Seton" now. His father had always insisted that this was their true family name as descendants of George Seton, Earl of Winton, but Mr Thompson never did find the time or the energy to have it changed himself. Ernest's action caused some bad feeling in the Thompson family and for a time he wrote under the pen-name "Seton-Thompson", which seemed to satisfy everybody. However, legally and by preference he was, from 1883 onward, "Ernest Thompson Seton".

One smoky October night while camping out in "Seton's Kingdom", Ernest watched the moon rise over a small lake, and recalled that only two years earlier he had looked at just such a moon shining down on the River Thames in London. It seemed like centuries ago that he had been a poor, sickly art student, living on beans and porridge. Now his health was robust, and he had land of his own and a little money. Best of all, he was doing what he wanted to do, observing the habits of birds and animals and well on the way to becoming a professional naturalist.

"So much for London and the art world," he said with satisfaction. "I guess I'm through with all that."

He found the Indian medicine bag where he kept his valuables and made a bonfire from the relics of his old life. As the letters from the Prince of Wales, the Archbishop of Canterbury and the Prime Minister, and even the Life Member's Ticket to the British Museum, went up in flames, he felt a great sense of release. It was as if his own insecure past was being burned up with the paper. He had found himself at last. From now on he was his own man and would go his own way.

But did his destiny lie here in the sandhills of Manitoba? He remembered his Voice, which had not predicted a future for him as a contented homesteader. Security was pleasant, but as a biologist, he knew that movement and activity were essential to life. And so, the very next month, on November 23, 1883, Ernest got off the train in New York with less than three dollars in his pocket and no clear idea of what he had come to do in the big city.

He soon found a room with an old friend from art school and a job making sketches for an advertising firm. Earlier that year he had published his first short nature story, "The Life of the Prairie Chicken", which had caught the attention of several editors, including Charles G. D. Roberts at *The Week* in Toronto. Encouraged by this interest, Seton began writing other stories, such as "Benny the Fox" and "The Snowshoe Rabbit", which found a ready market in the major magazines of the time. The reading public was tired of sentimental children's tales about animals and responded enthusiastically to Seton's well-written and scientifically accurate descriptions of the way animals really lived in the wild.

With the coming of spring, Seton grew restless with city life and decided to return to Canada. On the way back he visited Dr C. Hart Merriam, a well-known scientist, who had shown an interest in Seton's work.

"There's not an artist in America who can make a decent drawing of an animal," he told Seton. Then, taking a new species of shrew out of a bottle of alcohol, he dared Ernest to try his hand at it. The long years of artistic training and animal study came to Seton's aid, and within a few hours he produced a drawing which delighted Dr Merriam.

"This sketch alone gives you first place among all the animal illustrators on the continent," Merriam said. "I'd like fifty more like this, and I'll pay the highest prices for them."

Back in Toronto, Seton gave a speech to the Natural

History Society — the highlight of its annual meeting. Ernest was pleased with himself, and with good reason. At twenty-five, he was becoming successful in three different fields: writing, art, and natural science. Also, unlike the careers of most men, his work involved him in the kind of open-air life he enjoyed most.

The following years he spent on the prairies. He was working on notes for articles on the birds and mammals of Manitoba, adding page upon page to his journals, and finishing the pictures for Dr Merriam. There he met Chaska, a dignified Cree Indian who spoke English and became a good friend. Chaska guided him on many deer hunts and taught Seton much about woodcraft. Once Seton followed the trail of a moose for nineteen days, over three hundred miles on foot through heavy snow. He got his moose, but when the hunt was over, he looked at the splendid animal he had killed and thought: "Who am I to destroy such a creature simply for the pleasure of the hunt? I don't need the meat for food or the skin for clothing. At the rate they are being shot, soon all North America's big game animals will be extinct. I swear from this moment on I will never lift my rifle against any one of them again."

It was a vow he kept for the rest of his life. Moreover, the moose hunt provided him with the idea for his beautiful story, *The Trail of the Sandhill Stag*, which describes in almost religious terms the author's reverence for the spirit of nature. In it, a young hunter catches sight of a magnificent stag, and for many years searches to find it again. His respect for his quarry grows as he learns more about himself and the natural world. When he finally encounters the stag again, he does not shoot. Gazing into the animal's eyes, he feels a sense of the wisdom and mystery of creation, and acknowledges his own brotherhood with all living things.

In 1885, Seton made another trip to New York, where he drew animals for *The Century Dictionary*. Then it was back to Manitoba for several months, and after that, to Toronto, where he tried for his mother's sake to live at home in harmony with his father. But Mr Thompson was still not impressed with his son's achievements and Ernest soon realized that nothing had changed.

"If you're so famous, why can't you support your father as any normal son would do?" Mr Thompson would ask. "Where has all this nature business got you, after all? And don't forget, you still owe me some money for bringing you up."

Not surprisingly, Seton soon moved out of the family home and lived on his brother Joseph's farm near Lake Ontario, where he encountered many of the animals he would later make famous. Foxes had been making raids on Joseph's henhouse, and the angered hired hand had broken into a burrow, killing several pups and capturing one alive. This bewildered fox he chained in the yard, and the vixen devoted all her cunning to free her last child from captivity. She almost succeeded several times, and once lured Joseph's best hunting dog away to a nearby railway trestle, where he was smashed by an on-coming locomotive. Finally the mother brought her cub a chunk of poisoned meat — apparently preferring to see him die a wild fox than live in dishonour among humans. Most Seton fans would recognize this incident as the germ of "The Springfield Fox", one of the stories in *Wild Animals I Have Known*.

Joseph was forced to sell the farm, however, and Ernest had to conclude that Toronto was not meant to be his permanent place of residence. Before he left, he had the satisfaction of paying off the debt his father had never forgotten. As Mr Thompson solemnly entered "Paid" in his accounts book, Ernest began to feel sorry for the selfish old man who had been such a torment to him and the rest of the family. What a dreary life his father led, obsessed by his accounts book and refinement, and always distrustful of other people! Ernest was thankful that he had his freedom, his art, and, best of all, his love of nature to give life meaning and variety.

His next destination was Paris, at that time a world centre for artists of all kinds. Ernest felt somewhat uneasy and out of place in the art world there, however, and the famous delights of "Gay Paree" in the 1890's seemed to his mind silly and dull. He spent much of his time in the zoo — making studies for several large oil paintings of wolves, one of which was exhibited with honours at the Paris Salon in 1891.

The naturalist's zeal for accuracy is evident in Seton's paintings, for he went to great lengths to get every detail just right. Since dogs and wolves have similar anatomies, he began purchasing bodies from the Paris Dog Pound and carrying them back to his studio to dissect and sketch. Getting rid of the remains was a problem, since the health laws did not allow disposal of "pets" in garbage cans. So, in the still of the night, Seton would have to creep out and drop his grisly specimens over the bridge into the River Seine.

Paris at that time was rocked by the murder of a woman. The victim's body had not been found, but police suspected that her husband had been tossing bits of her into the river at intervals. One night, Seton went out with a particularly messy parcel, only to find the bridges crowded with gendarmes, who eyed his every move with intense interest. In desperation, he took the bundle back to his own street and tried to lose it forever in an open drain, but it got stuck somehow. It simply would not go down, and too late he realized that the wrapping had his own name and address on it. A policeman was strolling over to investigate, however, so he had to leave it where it was.

During the next few days, every knock at the door put Seton into a cold sweat. He could receive a heavy fine for violating health laws — or worse, the police might not realize that the thing in his conveniently addressed package was a dog. It would mean the Bastille, at least!

Brooding over the matter after a sleepless night, he happened to notice some familiar brown paper in the wastebasket. Yes, it was the same: he must have wrapped the dog in something else.

"Seton, it's a good thing you went into art," he said to himself, "because you would have been a failure as a criminal."

His concern for realism in art did not necessarily please the critics. A major canvas, *The Wolves' Triumph*, was rejected by the Paris Salon of 1892, because the subject matter was "offensive". The picture showed wolves feeding on a human corpse, and a Toronto selection committee also rejected it for the Canadian exhibit at the Chicago World's Fair: the judges felt it gave a false idea of life in Canada. Finally it was shown at the Fair, but only after a public controversy in which all the Toronto newspapers took sides on the work's artistic merits.

Seton made some lifelong friends in Paris and did important studies in the anatomy of animals, but eventually his "Buffalo Wind" began calling again. When he returned to Manitoba in 1892, he was struck by how much the land had changed since his first visit twelve years before. The true prairie was vanishing, ploughed under by farmers, and several species of birds and animals had vacated the area. The flatness of the plain was broken by farmhouses and towns, and the saplings Ernest had planted near the homestead at Carberry were now bushy shade trees. Many hundreds of small lakes had dried up or shrunk into reedy marshes, and the network of roads and fences over the countryside was further evidence that the west was no longer the wide-open frontier of Seton's youth.

But more had changed than the land. Seton himself, although only thirty-two, now suffered from attacks of arthritis, which meant that he could no longer stride over the plains like a young Indian brave. Even more serious was what the long years of painstaking work with pen and paintbrush had done to his eyesight. Special drawing boards and stronger glasses did not help, and finally his doctor said: "Seton, unless you want to go totally blind, you had better take a long vacation from your easel and all these feathers and claws you've been painting."

So in 1893, Seton accepted an invitation to a cattle ranch in New Mexico, from a man who hoped that an expert on wildlife could find some way to destroy a wolf pack that was killing his range stock. It was no easy task, since Lobo, the leader of the pack, had a reputation among the cowboys as a wolf of unusual strength and devilish cunning. Seton soon found that guns were useless, since Lobo was shrewd enough to avoid being seen by his enemies, although his howls were often heard echoing down the canyon, a full octave lower than the calls of the other wolves.

Lobo scorned Seton's poisoned baits, and either turned over or backed out of his most elaborate wolf traps. Then Seton learned that a small white she-wolf, called Blanca by the Mexican shepherds, was known to be Lobo's constant companion.

"Well, old fellow, I think I've got you now," Seton exclaimed to himself.

Managing to capture Blanca, he made tracks in the dirt with the dead wolf's paws. For once, Lobo threw caution to the winds and followed his mate's "trail" straight into a brace of traps. Struggling to escape the cruel metal jaws, he howled out to the pack, but this time they did not respond. Seton tried to lasso him now, but Lobo neatly bit the lasso in two and glared at his tormentor in defiance.

Seeing the great wolf in his hour of defeat, Seton could not bring himself to shoot, and with some difficulty brought Lobo back to the ranch house. There he was collared and chained to a stake in the pasture. Seton hoped that his call might bring more wolves into gunshot range, but Lobo did not make another sound.

He lay there quietly, indifferent to food and drink, his keen, yellow eyes fixed on the canyon opening which led to the plains beyond and freedom. Twenty-four hours later he was dead, his muzzle pointing to the canyon, and no wound on his body to explain the cause of his passing.

Seton was tremendously affected by Lobo's tragedy, and celebrated it in "Lobo, King of the Currumpaw". This story was his first major success, bringing him broad general recognition, and it is still one of his best-known works.

Seton's animal tales had been appearing regularly in magazines and papers throughout the 1890's, and in 1898 he offered a collection of them, along with his own illustrations, to Charles Scribner, the New York publisher. Scribner accepted, but said he could pay Seton only ten per cent of the published price of each book. "Most new books are financial failures, seldom selling more than a few hundred copies," he added. "Our offer may seem low to you, but a publisher has to cover his expenses."

"How many books must you sell to cover expenses, then?" Seton asked.

"Not less than two thousand copies."

"I am so sure of my book's future success that I will forgo *all* my profits on the first two thousand copies, provided you will *double* my share on every copy sold after that."

Scribner was taken aback, but he had to agree to these unusual terms since he had all but assured Seton his book would not sell. As Seton went out of the office, he was smiling, as if he had just set the perfect wolftrap. The first two thousand copies of the book, *Wild Animals I Have Known*, were sold out in the three weeks after publication, and soon the book became an international best seller. Seton's money worries were over.

He also received letters of congratulation from such well-known writers as Rudyard Kipling and Charles G. D. Roberts, who said that his work had greatly influenced their own writing. Seton followed this success with more popular favourites: *Lives of the Hunted, Biography of a Grizzly, Animal Heroes*, and many others.

In the Preface to *Wild Animals I Have Known*, he mentioned some of the things he wanted to do in his stories. First of all, each story was based on fact and described the personality of an individual animal which Seton had observed, usually in its natural setting. Since the stories were meant to be as realistic as possible, nobody lived happily ever after. "The life of a wild animal" Seton wrote, *"always has a tragic end."* He did not insist that the stories had any special moral lesson to teach, but hoped that his readers might come away with a better understanding of an animal's experience and of man's own kinship with the beasts.

As his books became widely read, Seton found himself in demand as a lecturer and after-dinner speaker. But every famous man has his critics, and in 1904 the respected American nature writer, John Burroughs, launched a vicious attack on Seton in *The Atlantic Monthly*, and denounced him as a fraud and a fake naturalist. Seton was shocked at this unexpected outburst, for he had admired Burroughs ever since coming upon his poetic descriptions of outdoor life many years before, in the British Museum.

One night at a dinner party, he spotted Burroughs, a handsome, white-haired old man, and asked the host to seat Burroughs next to him at the table. Seton later recorded their conversation in *Trail of an Artist-Naturalist*.

Burroughs looked nervous when he saw who his dining companion was, and he did not relax when Seton asked him politely: "Mr Burroughs, did you ever make a special study of wolves?"

"No," was the brief answer.

"Did you ever hunt wolves?"

"No."

"Did you ever photograph or draw wolves in a zoo?"

"No."

"Did you ever skin or dissect a wolf?"

"No."

"Did you ever live in wolf country?"

"No."

"Did you ever see a live wolf?"

"No."

"Then, by what rule of logic are you equipped to judge me, who have done all of these things hundreds of times?"

Burroughs tried to blurt out some kind of defence, and then directed the conversation to safer ground. But in the next issue of *The Atlantic Monthly*, Seton was delighted to see that the older man had printed a full apology for his attack. In return, Seton invited him to his home and took a slightly malicious pleasure in showing Burroughs his library filled with a thousand mammal skins, two thousand bird skins, photographs, drawings, and volumes of detailed journals.

"I've never seen such a collection before," exclaimed Burroughs. "Some of the things you have here I never dreamed existed. I have apologized publicly for my mistake, but please accept a private apology as well."

The men became close friends after this, but there was another, more important outcome to the Burroughs affair. Theodore Roosevelt, big-game hunter and amateur naturalist, who had become President of the United States, told Seton: "Burroughs and the people at large don't know how many facts you have back of your stories. You must publish your facts."

And so Seton, his eyes now strengthened by a miraculous pair of bi-focals, began work on a project which he published four years later as *Life Histories of Northern Mammals*. Ten years after this, Seton expanded the book into *Lives of Game Animals*, a scientific study in four volumes, which won almost every honour and medal available. By this time there could be no more question about Seton's credentials as a naturalist.

Highly successful in work, Seton was not quite so fortunate in his private life. In 1896, he married Grace Gallatin, a wealthy American girl he had met on the boat to Paris. They both had doubts about the marriage from the beginning, since Grace was fond of New York social life and fashionable literary parties, which bored Ernest to tears. Assuming that love would resolve all differences, the young couple set up housekeeping in Sloat Hall, a grim thirty-room mansion not far from New York City. Ernest worked all day drawing birds and wondering how he was ever going to pay for Sloat Hall, while Grace grew day by day more weary of quiet life in the country. The story that their monstrous house was haunted by the ghost of a murdered musician only strengthened her desire to move back to the city, even though Ernest proved that the ghost's "music" was only the wind blowing over some broken glass in the attic.

Grace had her way and the Setons returned to New York, where the wife blossomed and the husband grew restless and depressed. Finally they agreed to go their separate ways, although they did not get a divorce until 1937 when their daughter had married and settled down. The daughter, Anya Seton, became a well-known writer herself, the author of several best-selling novels.

With not altogether pleasant memories of Sloat Hall in his mind, Seton began looking for another kind of country place and found just what he wanted in an abandoned farm in a wilderness area of Connecticut. Here he hoped to carry out experiments in conservation and ecology, but a gang of neighbourhood boys considered that the property belonged to them. They declared war on Seton — sneaking up at night to destroy his fences, shoot his birds, and paint four-letter words on the rocks and trees. Friends told Seton he should have the gang arrested, an idea which shocked him.

"Do you want me to make jail-birds out of a group of young boys? Put yourself in their shoes. Here some stranger has come in to fence off the land they've used for hunting and fishing all their lives. And you tell me to throw them in with a cell-full of hardened criminals? No, let me handle this my own way."

One morning, he went to the village school and asked the teacher if he could talk to the boys for a few minutes.

"Boys, you know who I am, and I know you. I'm here to invite you to a camp-out on my property next Friday. It will last the entire weekend, and I'll provide the boats, tents and all the grub you can eat. The only rules are: no rifles, no matches, no tobacco, and no whisky. Will you be there?"

The boys stared at him suspiciously and no one said a word.

"There's nothing to pay," Seton added, feeling less sure of himself. "And no strings attached. Is it yes or no?"

The only answer was a stony silence.

"Well, remember, next Friday at four o'clock."

At four that Friday Seton and the cook he had hired waited by the piles of food and heaps of camping equipment, but no boys appeared.

"I tell you, Mr Seton, this bunch of kids is no good," said the cook. "The only thing that'll set them straight is a rawhide strap, well laid on in the right place."

Seton, remembering how little his father's riding crop had done for him, smiled and shook his head.

"They'll be here," he said calmly.

And at five o'clock, exactly an hour late, the boys came in a group, whooping and hollering; forty-two of them, over twice as many as Seton had expected.

"Hey mister, what are we supposed to do?"

"Is this some kind of trick?"

First Seton let them work off their energy running through the woods and swimming in the lake he had made by draining a swamp. Then he stuffed them with food and watched an entire weekend's supplies vanish in an hour; luckily, the next day was a Saturday and the stores would be open. As the boys sat around the campfire in the twilight, tired but happy, Seton decided the right moment had come.

"Now shall I tell you a story?"

"Sure," they said politely, "go ahead."

Then Seton began to tell of the life of the Plains Indians, making each anecdote more exciting than the one before. As readers all over the world knew, he was a master storyteller, and soon had the group following his every word with breathless interest. Finally, when he had finished his most dramatic tale about a spy in an enemy Indian's camp, Seton said: "Well, it's time to get some sleep. Look, are we going to camp out here like a pack of tramps, or shall we do it Indian style?"

"Indian style!" came the thundering response.

Seton helped the boys elect a Chief and a Council of Twelve to head their tribe, and suggested for himself the post of Medicine Man and advisor. As the weekend slipped by, he taught them to make campfires without matches, to measure the width of a river without crossing it, and a number of other outdoor skills. The boys wanted to wear feathers in their hair, so a system of winning feathers for achievements in nature study and woodcraft was invented. The boys learned to set up teepees and to shoot bows and arrows at a wooden deer Seton rigged up as a target to protect the wildlife. His experiment was a huge success. At last his own childhood dream of leading an Indian tribe had come true, and as for the boys, they had the time of their life.

"Look at them," he told the cook. "They are governing themselves, learning useful skills, improving their health, and having fun into the bargain. And these are the boys everybody wanted me to throw into jail!"

News of the weekend spread around the countryside, and Seton was encouraged to write a series of articles on his methods and theories for the *Ladies' Home Journal* in 1902. This started the growth of the Woodcraft Movement in the United States, a national organization which later developed into the Boy Scouts.

In 1906, Seton lectured on the Woodcraft Movement in England, and suggested that something similar should be started there. General Robert Baden-Powell was called in as an organizer. Baden-Powell was a military man and his life in the army naturally influenced his ideas on scouting, which were very different from Seton's concern for imitating the Indian. The military quality of the British movement gained popularity in the American scouting organization, although Seton himself was Chief Scout from 1910 to 1915, and wrote the first American scout manual.

"We're not training the boys to become soldiers," he complained to the board of directors. "We want them to become men through close experience with life in the woods, not weigh them down with badges and khaki uniforms. The Indian, not the army general, should be our ideal."

But the directors disagreed, and after a secret meeting of the board, Seton was told that he was no longer a member of the organization he had done so much to bring into existence. It was a cruel blow, but he survived it. When friends asked why he didn't write an attack on the board of directors, he would only shrug his shoulders and say: "Scouting is too important to ruin with any bad publicity. The majority has decided that my way was not what they wanted, and there is no point in making a fuss about it."

Aside from this bitter disappointment, the last portion of Seton's life was a peaceful and happy time. Already known throughout the world for his writings and lectures, he added to his fame in 1907 by discovering the Earl Grey River in the Canadian Arctic, an area he described vividly in his book, *The Arctic Prairies.*

After his divorce from Grace he married again, although this time he did not make the mistake of choosing a woman who did not really share his interests. He was lucky in the second Mrs Seton, Julia Buttree, who had been his secretary for many years. She was herself a writer, who did studies of North American Indians.

They settled down on a twenty-five hundred acre tract of wilderness land in New Mexico, where they built a large adobe house which the neighbours nicknamed "Seton Castle". Here Seton wrote several more animal biographies, including *The Biography of an Arctic Fox* and *Santana, the Hero Dog of France.* He also collected the notes and drawings for his useful *Animal Tracks and Hunter Signs,* which Julia Seton assembled into a book after his death. When he was seventy-eight, he became the father of another daughter, Beulah, who at an early age travelled with her parents on lecture tours and performed Indian dances in costume.

As he grew older, Seton became convinced that modern man was destroying himself through his indifference to nature. He spent much of his time promoting a return to the outdoors, and in the 1930's, Seton Castle became Seton Institute, devoted to the study of nature and Indian lore. For a time this was the centre for the new Woodcraft League of America, where Seton taught the ideals of the original Woodcraft Movement.

Perhaps Seton's own life was the best proof of his philosophy. As a child he had been sickly and cross-eyed, and more than once the doctors had wondered if he would recover from his various illnesses. Poor diet and overwork had often threatened his body and an unsympathetic father had threatened his spirit. In nature, whether it was on the Manitoba prairies or in the ravines near Toronto, Seton could regain his health, cheer his spirits, and eventually find his life's work.

Busy and active until the end of his life, Seton spent long hours hiking with his wife over the rugged New Mexico hills, always on the alert for something new to jot down in his notebook. He died peacefully on October 23, 1946, at the age of eighty-six.

# Sir Charles G. D. Roberts

It was a silent midwinter morning, and as Charlie Roberts climbed up the pasture hill the snow collapsed with dry, sharp crunches under his hurrying footsteps. He turned impatiently to Dave, his father's hired man, who was struggling to keep up.

"Oh come on, Dave. Don't you want to see if we snared anything?"

"I can see there's no holding back a great hunter," puffed Dave, glad to slow down the pace for a chat. "But don't you worry. If any of them rabbits got into our traps, they won't be rushing away any too soon."

But his words were wasted breath, for Charlie had already gone on to the crest of the hill and was moving into a grove of ice-crusted fir trees. He had never felt this way before: almost dizzy with a strange, keen-edged eagerness to see if his traps had worked. The day before, Dave had taught him how to bend down the young saplings, lock them in place with spliced twigs, and fasten slender nooses of copper wire to the ends. Charlie had made three snares, and surely one of them must have snapped up an unsuspecting rabbit during the night.

He watched the ground carefully, picking out the dotted lines of small-animal tracks criss-crossing the crisp snow. Then he noticed the larger snowshoe prints of a rabbit, and almost broke into a run to reach the clearing.

"Dave! We did it!"

From his vantage point, Charlie could see the saplings, two of them bowed down by dangling shapes that looked like miniature hanged men. But as he walked towards the third, unsuccessful trap, his feeling of triumph began to ebb. The snow beneath the sprung snare was spattered with blood, and lying close by was the hideous chewed-off head of a rabbit.

"Reckon a fox got to that bunny before we did," said Dave, when he finally reached the spot. "Gnawed his head clean away to get the body out of the noose. Happens sometimes. Other ones are all right, though."

"Do you think the rabbit was still alive when it happened?" Charlie asked dully, staring at the scene. He was feeling a bit green around the gills.

"Could be. Mother Nature can be a cruel old lady. Well, come on, thought you was in a big hurry. We got chores to do before breakfast."

Reluctantly, Charlie cut down one of the other rabbits from its tight, copper noose. The furred body was frozen stiff as a board, the dead eyes looked blankly at nothing, and the small tongue jutted out through strangely delicate teeth. Charlie's excitement had been replaced by a kind of despair. While making the traps, he had never thought of the rabbits as being alive.

Suddenly Charlie dropped the corpse in the snow.

"Hey butterfingers," Dave called, the last rabbit now strung professionally over his shoulders, "what's got into you?"

As Dave watched in open-mouthed amazement, Charlie went to each of the snares and kicked them down. Then he said without a trace of emotion: "O.K., Dave, that's the end of trapping for me. You can have both rabbits."

Back in the Roberts dining room, Charlie sat sulkily in his place as his mother, a small, lively woman, set the table for breakfast.

"What in the world are you doing down here so early?" she asked. "Didn't you get your rabbit?"

"Yes, but...I gave it to Dave," he muttered. Now that it was over, the incident was beginning to embarrass him. He wasn't a child any more, and many people might think it stupid or unmanly to get so upset over a dead rabbit. He hoped Dave wouldn't tell anyone.

"I must say, I was surprised that you took up this trapping business," his mother said, reaching around him to deal out the porridge bowls. "You always were a great one for animals. Remember when you were three, and put my wedding rings on those dead mice? You said you were bringing them back to life. Those rings smelled funny for days afterwards. I swear, I was half ashamed to take my gloves off in public."

She began to laugh, and even in the depths of his depression, Charlie couldn't help but smile. He had heard the story a million times, but his mother always knew how to make people see the brighter side of life.

"Well, that's the sickliest smile I ever did see, Charlie Roberts. Whatever's wrong with you, you march right in and talk it over with your father. He's in the study — writing a sermon. And don't let me see that sour face of yours again, until your temper's sweetened. Now, get."

Charlie entered his father's study without knocking, for the Reverend George Goodridge Roberts was by no means one of those frosty Victorian ministers who stood on ceremony. A tall, robust sportsman, he was an expert on every subject under the sun, and loved nothing better than passing his knowledge on to others. Everything George Roberts did seemed to be transformed by his own enthusiasm: he enjoyed politics, sermon-writing, farming, and anything to do with books. But most of all he enjoyed coaching his son in gymnastics, reading aloud to him from the classics, and helping him out in painting, music, and writing poetry. Throughout his life, Charlie would say that his best friend had always been his father.

"You made an important decision today," Mr Roberts said, after hearing his son's story. "It was a courageous decision, in fact, and I can't see what you're ashamed of. There's a case to be made for hunting animals, of course — for food, for protection, and for sport. But killing rabbits for the fun of it is poor sport in my opinion."

"Everybody does it around here."

"If *that's* going to be the motto which guides you on the rocky road of life, you're in for a lot of trouble," his father said with a broad smile.

"I didn't mean it that way. The thing is, I enjoy hunting down animals, and yet I feel guilty about it. I like to be out in nature as much as anyone."

"Of course! You come from a family of naturalists, as you know," boomed Mr Roberts, rising from his chair in his enthusiasm for the subject. "Your uncle is a fine botanist, almost a professional, and I have long made nature my particular study. But you don't have to trap nature or shoot it to pieces in order to know it well."

Charlie tried to explain the great excitement he had felt in going to the traps that morning.

"Every man knows that primitive feeling. Our ancestors were hunters. Indeed, some scientists believe that we are descended from the beasts themselves. Is it any wonder that we feel such savage delight in the hunt?" Mr Roberts relaxed again, settling into his chair.

"But men have reason and charity. They can exercise control over their untamed selves. Killing rabbits for killing's sake is not very reasonable."

"I guess not."

At that moment, the sun broke through the winter haze outside and lit up the gold lettering on the backs of George Roberts' leather-bound books. Charlie realized that he felt much better, although he had another question.

"And if I catch other people killing for killing's sake?"

The Reverend George Roberts looked up at his strapping son, one of the best athletes in the parish, and said with gentle good humour: "Christian reason works wonders, but don't forget that God did not absolutely forbid such a thing as righteous anger."

Charlie laughed out loud at this, and his father joined in. Good-natured laughter was often to be heard in the Roberts household, and Charles' early life goes a long way to disprove the theory that every writer has an unhappy childhood. Born in 1860, he grew up in Westcock Parsonage, New Brunswick, where his father was in charge of a large parish which included the town of Sackville.

The parsonage was situated in a pleasant, rural area, the minister's property including a comfortable house and a farm, where Charlie worked with the other help, harvesting marsh hay, bee-keeping, and tending the animals. The house was usually bustling with activity, with all the dogs and cats, and Charlie's brother and sister, and the uncounted numbers of Maritime relatives who often dropped in for a visit.

Westcock is in the Tantramar marsh country, where

long dikes hold back the powerful tides of the Bay of Fundy from flooding the lush acreage of grassland. The lonely, haunting beauty of this landscape was to be described often in Roberts' poetic works, as in his famous poem, "Tantramar Revisited":

Miles on miles they extend, level, and grassy, and dim,
Clear from the long red sweep of flats to the sky in the distance,
Save for the outlying heights, green-rampired Cumberland Point;
Miles on miles outrolled, and the river-channels divide them —
Miles on miles of green, barred by the hurtling gusts.

Despite the many travels of his later life, Roberts never really left the Tantramar as far as his imagination was concerned, and much of his best writing may be traced back to his youthful experience in the area.

He often explored the woods and marshes with his uncle, Dr Edward Roberts, an avid fisherman who taught Charlie a great deal about plants and animals. Edward is probably the original of Uncle Andy in *Babes of the Wild* (published in the United States as *Children of the Wild*), in which an older man tells tales about animals and their young to a boy named Babe. Babe is a bit of a ninny in the book, but Charlie Roberts himself was a proficient student with a memory like a steel trap.

As for more formal education, his father was his only teacher until he was fourteen, and a more congenial atmosphere for learning than Westcock Parsonage was probably never granted to anybody. The lessons were like friendly conversations, and yet Charlie, almost without noticing, got swept along by his father's interest into a solid training in Latin, Greek, French, algebra and geometry.

The Reverend George Roberts was also an earnest patriot, who strongly supported Canadian Confederation. One of Roberts' most vivid memories was of the day he and his father were riding through the bright, summer woods when they heard church bells tolling in the distance. Mr Roberts reined in the horses and looked his boy straight in the eye.

"Do you know what those bells mean, Charlie? This is the day your homeland becomes a nation. It's a proud thing to be alive at the birth of a new country, and I only hope you will grow up to play your part in this united Canada."

Few people around the Tantramar doubted that such a talented, athletic, and popular boy as Charlie Roberts would amount to something eventually. At the tender age of twelve he was writing agricultural articles professional enough to get published in *The Colonial Farmer*, a Fredericton journal. Wanting to meet his editor, Charles had his father take him into the city for a visit. George Roberts introduced himself to the gaunt, lantern-jawed Maritimer at the desk, but before he could say more, the editor said: "Glad to meet you, Reverend Roberts. Fine articles you wrote on the cattle and the Houdan fowl. Particularly liked 'Composts for Upland Farms'."

"Oh, but I didn't write...," began Mr Roberts.

"I'm a plain-spoken man, and I don't often praise a man to his face." The editor allowed himself a wintry little smile. "But I like your work and I hope we'll be seeing more of it."

"Well sir, the man you want to be praising is my son here," said Mr Roberts proudly. "I had nothing to do with any of it. Here is the author of 'Composts for Upland Farms', and all the others too."

Charles pulled off his cap and stepped forward, but the editor only stared, pursing his lips together so fiercely that his mouth almost disappeared.

"How old is he?" asked the editor, after an uncomfortable silence.

"Only twelve," Mr Roberts replied, beaming with satisfaction.

"Mumph," grunted the editor, clearly scandalized that his august newspaper had been publishing the work of such an infant. He froze Charlie with a glance, and then turned without another word to ask Mr Roberts about weather conditions on the Bay of Fundy.

Visits to the city were few and far between, however, and most of Charlie's time was taken up with farm work and family gatherings and Church services, where he played the organ loudly enough to drown out the choir when it went astray. Wandering through the woods and marshland, he observed the animals which featured in his writing many years afterwards. The incident of the rabbit snares was the inspiration behind "The Moonlight Trails", the first tale in *Kindred of the Wild*, and it is likely that many of Roberts' stories involving the Boy and an animal had some basis in his Tantramar days.

One evening in the forest, for example, he ran smack into a now-rare Eastern Canadian lynx, which the New Brunswickers called a "lucifee". Charlie stood stock-still in terror as the big smoke-coloured cat padded around him, examining the alien human with glittering eyes. A sudden squeak from a new pair of shoes made the creature vanish, and for weeks afterwards Charlie tested his knowledge of woodcraft by playing a dangerous game of hide-and-seek with the elusive lynx. This was to be the kernel of one of Roberts' finest tales, "The Haunter of the Pine Gloom".

Life in the Tantramar was bound to the necessary work of the farm and the slow rhythmic changes of the seasons, but it was never dull. During one storm, the powerful Fundy tides broke through the dikes and carried far inland an old, sunken ship dragged up from the bottom of the sea. Charlie and the other children played Robinson Crusoe around the wreck for years afterwards, and as an adult Roberts wrote a poem about it, "The Stranded Ship".

Tragedy could break through the placid surface of New Brunswick life in unexpected ways. One day Charlie and his father went to a neighbour's barn to borrow a hoe, only to find the neighbour himself hanging from the rafters by a rope — a suicide. Years later, Roberts thought he saw a body swaying again in the same barn and forced himself to investigate. There was no dead man, but — needless to say — the event was used in a short story, "The Barn on the Marsh".

And so the Tantramar days passed, with Charlie enjoying good health, a sound education, a happy family, and continual contact with the outdoors. It was almost a storybook childhood, too good to be true, and it could not last forever. In 1874, the Reverend George Roberts was promoted. He now became rector of the parish of Fredericton, and the family moved from Westcock Parsonage.

Charlie, of course, was sad to leave the marsh

country, but Fredericton was a beautiful little city surrounded by woods, and as the new minister's son he was made to feel welcome. As everywhere in New Brunswick, there was a network of relatives and good friends living in town, including Roberts' cousin, Bliss Carman, a boy of his own age. Like Charles Roberts he was destined to become one of Canada's foremost poets. Certainly there was none of the misery for Roberts here that Seton had to undergo in his move from Lindsay to Toronto.

He entered Fredericton Collegiate School at the age of fourteen, two years earlier than usual, and soon went to the head of the class, thanks to the standard of his father's teaching. His high-school career was almost unreasonably successful. With little trouble, he won the highest marks and the biggest awards; he was active in athletics and the leader of a secret social fraternity. It is easy for The Perfect Student to turn into The Perfect Prig, hated by everyone, but Roberts was saved by his humour and sense of proportion.

Also, he was stubborn. The way he learned to swim indicates his practical approach to the problems of life in general. After almost drowning in the St John River, he studied closely the movements he saw the other swimmers make, and then practised them alone on dry land. For days he would wade into the water up to his chest and try to make it back to shore. After a week of sinking, struggling, and spitting out river water, he mastered the basics and was ready to go on to the fancier strokes. In a month, he was an expert.

Charlie entered the University of New Brunswick (in Fredericton) in 1876, at the age of sixteen, and graduated three years later. Predictably, he distinguished himself in every sphere of campus life, but an important part of his education took place in the country outside Fredericton. There he met many woodsmen who could teach him the lore of the forest and the elements of woodcraft. He was to find roles for these men — hunters, trappers, lumberjacks, hobos, and eccentrics — in the fiction of his adult years.

Summers were spent on full-scale canoe trips in the Madawaska region north of the city, where there were fascinating river islands for camping, exploring, and inventing tall tales about. Roberts used one of these excursions as the framework for his book, *Around the Campfire*, where each member of a canoe trip tells stories about a wilderness experience. The "Queerman" in the book is meant to be Bliss Carman, already known at school for his eccentric clothes and his carefree philosophy that a vagabond has the best life.

During his college years, Charles fell in love with Mary Fenety, daughter of the Queen's Printer for New Brunswick. Mary's father was a man who fervently believed in himself, and who had a way of forcing his opinions on other people as if he were broadcasting the gospel truth. Most people let him have his way, but Charlie believed in his own worth too, and was never one to hide his light under a bushel. It was inevitable that these two would cross swords some day, and it happened one afternoon at Sunday dinner, when Charles dared to contradict Mr Fenety's statements about a religious point.

"I beg your pardon, sir, but you're wrong."

"Wrong, am I?" Mr Fenety laid down his knife and

fork, astounded. "And I suppose you are an authority? I suppose you have read Bishop Whately's argument on this subject? And McNair's book?"

"I have," said Roberts, the parson's son, "and also Dr Thorne's rebuttal."

Then Charles began to set the old man right, but Mr Fenety did not take kindly to instruction and at last jumped up, slammed down his chair, and stomped out of the dining room.

"Well Charlie, now you've done it," said Mary with a reproachful look. "I guess I won't be seeing much more of you."

Even gentle Mrs Fenety murmured that Charles had better be leaving, since her husband was not used to other points of view being expressed in his household.

"But that's just what he wanted," Charles said, serenely finishing his dinner. "He's been aching for an argument all day. You'll find that he likes me a thousand times better after this."

And, a few minutes later, Mr Fenety did poke his head in the doorway and remark: "Charlie, I'm going for my walk now. Don't you feel like coming along and having more discussion?"

So Roberts became fast friends with the man who was to become his father-in-law and who would be financing the publication of his first book. He had been jotting verses for a long time, but now he was writing poetry in earnest and getting some of it published in major magazines. In fact, his reputation as a poet was already so great in New Brunswick that when he graduated from University and took up a post as headmaster of the Chatham Grammar School, his students were expecting a famous old man with a flowing beard and world-wide fame. They were surprised to find that the new principal was nineteen, only a few years older than themselves. But Roberts had managed the beard, although it wasn't exactly flowing. He had nurtured it specially over the summer to make sure his classes would treat him with the respect due to age.

He didn't have to worry. The students listened in hushed silence when he read Shelley or Browning aloud, or explained the beauties of Latin verse. Always athletic, he also joined in the students' games and paddled along with them on canoe trips. His classes worshipped him, and their adoration only increased when his first book of poetry appeared in the autumn of 1880. He was just twenty years old.

The book was *Orion and Other Poems*, one of the most important books of poetry ever to appear in Canada, not so much for its content as for its influence on other poets in the young nation. Archibald Lampman, for example, stayed up all night reading and re-reading *Orion*, and later wrote:

> It seemed to me a wonderful thing that such a work could be done by a Canadian, by a young man, one of ourselves. It was like a voice from some new paradise of art calling to us to be up and doing.

Archibald Lampman, along with Bliss Carman and Duncan Campbell Scott, were among the "Confederation Poets" to be inspired by Roberts' example. *Orion* proved to them that a poet did not have to be British or American to write well, that a Canadian literature was possible, and that the new nation should be able to produce a fresh and characteristic kind of poetry.

*Orion* received praise from the critics too, and Roberts was now determined to devote his life to literature. Jubilant with success, he married Mary Fenety in December 1880. But first volumes by young poets don't pay many bills. Expenses increased in 1882, when Mary gave birth to a boy, Athelstan. Later that same year Roberts moved from Chatham to a better-paying job as headmaster of a school in Fredericton. He drove himself to write as much as possible, turning out essays on all sorts of topics, as well as poetry. Teaching, which had seemed a high-spirited game in Chatham, daily became more and more of a grind, and Roberts wrote Bliss Carman that it was draining away all his energy for creative work.

In 1883, when an offer arrived from Toronto to edit a new journal devoted to the cultural advancement of Canada, Roberts snapped it up. He moved his wife and children to the city — hoping that this would be the break he'd been waiting for. But somehow nothing seemed to work out. To begin with, Toronto has never been at its best in November, the month Roberts arrived, and the drizzly weather oppressed his spirits. He did manage to publish the work of some fine young Canadians in his journal, *The Week*, but he had to work himself to a nub to get the paper out on time and was forced to write most of it himself. But worst of all, he could not get along with *The Week*'s owner, Goldwin Smith.

Smith was an Englishman who had grown disgusted

with the class system in his own country and saw American democracy as the hope for mankind. Therefore he hoped that Canada would turn its back on Britain and eventually become annexed to the United States — an idea he naturally wanted publicized in the columns of his newspaper.

"But Mr Smith, with all respect, we are Canadians," said Roberts, having a sip of sherry at "The Grange", his boss's home, which was like an English lord's mansion except for the Canadian landscape just beyond the windowpanes. "Our only future greatness lies in complete independence."

Goldwin Smith looked at him with an amused smile. "My dear Roberts, independence is an attractive fantasy, but the economic facts alone...."

Roberts followed his host into a sitting room filled with fine rosewood furniture imported direct from London. He warned himself not to get into another argument and not to stay much longer. *The Week* had to go to the printer's the next day and there was a mountain of work left to do. But as Smith's cultivated voice flowed on about the advantages of becoming American, Roberts forgot his good intentions.

"Economic facts are not the only things men live for," he said sharply.

"But let me explain to you about the spirit of Democracy as Jefferson conceived of it...."

"Jefferson was not a Canadian."

Soon they were in a spirited argument, the sort that Roberts had once enjoyed very much with his father-in-law. But now he was very tired. With a small sigh, he noticed that the winter sky was growing darker outside

JARVIS ST. COLLEGIATE, FEB. 5, 1925

Charles G. D. Roberts

Canadian Recital Tour
1925

*From a newspaper
cartoon by
T. E. Powers,
May 24, 1907
(see page 91)*

*Illustration by
Charles Livingston Bull
from Roberts'
Red Fox, 1905*

*Illustration by
Paul Bransom
from Roberts'
The Feet of
the Furtive, 1912*

and that a cold, thin rain was seeping down over Toronto. As usual, he would have to stay up all night to get *The Week* out.

The situation was impossible. After four months as editor, Roberts left *The Week*. Smith gave him a full year's salary, but this would soon run out, and then what? He took a brief trip to New York, to look for another editorial post, but found nothing. He made inquiries for an opening in the Civil Service at Ottawa, but again there was nothing. Without too many regrets at leaving Toronto, he moved the family back to Fredericton, where, to make matters worse, his health broke down and he contracted typhoid fever. Illness did nothing to brighten his outlook on the future, which suddenly began to look grim and frightening.

Roberts was now twenty-four. He was one of the most famous literary men in Canada, but he was also jobless and worried. He tried to live by free-lance writing for a time, but although editors liked his work, occasional payments from the magazines were not enough to keep his family from starvation. After his golden youth, Roberts was not used to failure and this black period of insecurity scared him. It may help to explain why he worked so hard for the rest of his life, even when he was financially well off. This period didn't last long, however, and in 1885 he was offered a professorship at King's College in Windsor, Nova Scotia. Needless to say, Roberts forgot his reservations about teaching and accepted on the spot.

He spent ten years at King's College as professor of literature. He had his classes arranged so they would be over by noon, and this gave him the rest of the day to write. During these years he produced a flood of essays, poems, histories, lectures, translations, and stories; he wrote an article on Nova Scotian railroad construction, translated a historical novel about Quebec, and put together a tourist guidebook to Eastern Canada. His ability to work on almost any subject was remarkable, but it is probably true that Roberts wrote too much, and spread his talent too thin. He knew that his poetry was more important than tourist guidebooks and translations, but he also knew that poetry did not pay the rent. "I live *for* poetry *by* prose," he remarked many years later.

At Windsor he did write some of his most lasting poems, including *Songs of the Common Day*, sonnets which express the moods and scenes of the Tantramar country. He also continued to write his patriotic verses, which used to be more widely read than they are now. The most famous one of these begins:

O Child of Nations, giant-limbed
  Who stand'st among the nations now
Unheeded, unadored, unhymned,
  With unanointed brow; —

How long the ignoble sloth, how long
  The trust in greatness not thine own?
Surely the lion's brood is strong
  To front the world alone!

Roberts' vision of the exact way in which Canada should "front the world alone" changed during his years as a professor. He began by believing that his country should strive for complete independence from Britain and scorned any other proposal, especially Goldwin Smith's plan for American annexation. But his father convinced him that the best way for Canada was a semi-independent status within the British Empire, and much of his political verse was based on a belief which Roberts phrased this way: "A good Canadian Nationalist *must* be a good British Imperialist."

Almost all the things Roberts ever wrote, from nature poems to histories to tourist guidebooks, were united by one common theme: Canada. His patriotism went far beyond his fervent interest in the nation's political future, for he was fascinated by the land as a unique place with its own special spirit and beauty. He hoped to capture this special quality in his writing.

His chest-thumping imperialist verses couldn't be more out of style today, most readers preferring the quiet poems on New Brunswick landscapes. Even these seem old-fashioned to some, but whatever is decided about the value of Roberts' poetry, there can be no doubt about his importance as the first poet to see the possibilities of Canada as a literary subject.

One morning as he walked back from a class at King's College, Roberts noticed two boys dropping stones on a large garter snake held fast to the ground by a forked stick.

"Here, what's this?" he said gruffly, dropping his Latin textbook and grabbing the nearest boy's arm.

The boy looked surprised.

"Can't you see, sir? We're breaking its back, so's it can't move," he said, as if explaining to a two-year-old. "Then we leave it out in the sun and it bakes to death."

Too shocked to speak for a moment, Roberts studied the faces before him and had to admit they were no different from the faces of any other decent, ordinary boys.

"But why on earth should you want to torment such a splendid creature?" he asked finally.

The boys laughed as if the professor had made a very funny joke.

"Sir, now, don't you know snakes are poison?"

"There are no poisonous snakes in Nova Scotia, and even if this were a king cobra, there would be no reason to torture it in such a savage fashion."

The boys were silent for a minute, and then one said: "Aw, we were just having some fun."

"*Fun!*"

His father's advice about righteous anger echoed through Roberts' mind, and he decided it was time to end the lecture. After some brisk words and well-aimed swats from a heavy Latin book, the boys were more than willing to leave their victim, and Roberts quickly put the snake out of its agony.

"How savage men can be," he thought as he walked on. "From the beasts' point of view we humans must seem the most vicious race on earth. And yet those boys were not being consciously wicked."

His meditations on the cruelty in nature and on man's role in the natural order of things were soon to bear fruit in his writing.

For many readers, the most important thing Roberts wrote during his years at King's College was his first animal story, "Do Seek Their Meat From God". In it, a five-year-old boy is threatened by two hungry panthers in an empty cabin. The boy's father saves him in the nick of time, and shoots the beasts, although Roberts shows us that the panthers are not evil monsters, but natural parents searching for food. Several weeks later, the father finds the panther's cave and the bodies of the two cubs who starved to death because their parents had not returned. This short, gripping tale suggests the hard laws of nature: a human child is saved, but only at the expense of two animal children.

Roberts had trouble getting the story published, since its bleak ending and its sympathy for dangerous animals were unusual at the time. Cautious editors returned it with puzzled comments, and *Harper's* magazine only accepted it at last with many doubts and misgivings. He tried a few more tales of the kind but stopped when editors offered no encouragement. It was much later, after the success of Seton's *Wild Animals I Have Known*, that Roberts began writing animal stories in quantity.

While at King's College, Roberts also entered a Dominion-wide competition for writing a history of Canada. His history did not win, although it later was published and became fairly popular. But the judges did not like it. The reason? It was too interesting! One judge was even overheard saying in a serious voice: "You know, if we assigned this Roberts history as a textbook, children might become too intrigued with the events and forget they are studying History as a subject." Another entry, written by a Supreme Court Judge from British Columbia, proved to be so outstandingly boring and dry that the committee awarded it the prize with pleasure.

Naturally Roberts could not work all the time, and the house at Windsor, like his old family home at Westcock, was often bustling with visits and parties. His parlour became a magnet for authors from all over the world. Sometimes the assembled group would play a verse-writing game in which each person had to write something on a given subject within a time limit. Another favourite pastime was experimenting with ESP, and the player who was It tried to find a hidden object with the help of thought waves transmitted by the others. Roberts also learned how to cast horoscopes, and for awhile he and his friends tried receiving messages from the Beyond through a Ouija board, until the Beyond started giving out nonsense advice and swearing at the guests.

Throughout his life, Roberts was fascinated by the occult, and once, in Germany, he was even visited by the ghost of a little girl who had committed suicide in a room he was renting. She was invisible, but every night Roberts felt her presence in the doorway and the touch of her cold hand stroking his forehead. He was not afraid, but the girl's frozen fingers got to be a nuisance and he was relieved to find that leaving the light on all night discouraged her. His interest in mysteries and coincidences shows up in several of his stories, one of the finest being "The Perdu", which concerns a strange pool and a greenish hand which seems to emerge from its unearthly depths.

In 1895, Roberts resigned from King's College. Despite the security of his job and the charm of the small Nova Scotia town, he longed for a change, and teaching had never been his first love. The mass of writing done in Windsor had established him firmly as a writer, and in 1893 he had been elected a Fellow of the Royal Society of Literature. Now he felt sure he could earn a living through his creative work and he returned to Fredericton with plans for building a house there. Now with three children to support, he soon increased his already high literary productivity. For example, in 1896 alone he published two volumes of short stories, as well as *The Forge in the Forest*, the first of his many historical novels about Acadia, the land of Evangeline.

He was doing well enough in Fredericton, but was growing very restless. When an offer to become assistant editor of *The Illustrated American* came in 1897, he was just in the mood to take it and move to New York City — leaving his wife and children at home. It was a more drastic step than perhaps Roberts realized at the time. He was not to return permanently to Canada for another twenty-five years, and apart from brief visits and vacations, he did not see a great deal of his family during that time. However, he supported Mary and the children until his wife's death in 1930, and this doubled the financial strain.

How was it that such a dedicated Canadian and family man would make such a move? Nobody knows exactly. Perhaps Roberts just wanted to conquer larger worlds than Fredericton had to offer, or realized that he would need publishing contacts outside Canada in order to survive. It is also plain that his marriage was fraying at the seams. Like Seton, Roberts had married young and impetuously, discovering too late that he and his wife had very little in common.

Roberts soon became a name to be reckoned with in the literary and publishing circles of New York. He lived with his cousin Bliss Carman, and their social set was a lively bohemian crowd of poets, painters, and editors. It was not long before he was a member of the Authors' Club of America and a charter member of the National Institute of Arts and Letters. He still worked with unflagging patience — writing everything from essays on battleships to light-hearted love poetry, from philosophical sonnets to Acadian romances like *A Sister to Evangeline*.

He was also learning what it meant to be a Canadian abroad. On bone-chilling December days, his New York friends would be surprised that he bothered to put on a scarf and coat.

"This weather down here must seem hot to you, compared with what you're used to," they would say with all sincerity.

"Oh, I like a southern climate," Roberts would remark, stamping his feet to ward off frost-bite.

"Do the polar bears give you much trouble up there? Aren't they quite dangerous?"

"No, in New Brunswick they come up to the cabin and eat right out of our hands. They aren't used to men yet, you see, and are still tame."

"Well, how about that! You know, it's curious, but I always expected that a Canadian would dress differently."

"We do at home, but it's too warm for my buffalo robe and Mountie hat down here," Roberts said drily. It was one thing to be the acknowledged expert on all things Canadian in a foreign country, and another thing to have people always expecting to meet a trapper in buckskins."

Perhaps it was in reaction to this that he began

wearing a *pince-nez*, small eyeglasses that clip directly on the nose, which he attached to the inside of his vest with a heavy black ribbon. It became his trademark, along with the extreme formality of his clothing: a starched collar, spats, bow-tie, waistcoat, and walking stick. In his photographs there is usually a sober, stand-offish look on his face and he must have upset many an American's image of what the average Canadian looked like.

In the years away from home, Roberts' life might seem to have been designed by a travel agent. His professional base was New York, but he lived at various times in London, France, and Germany, as well as making trips to Cuba, Italy, Algeria, and many other parts of the world. On these wanderings he might be accompanied by one of his sons, a brother, or his cousin, and he had a wide circle of friends. But Roberts gives the impression of having been a lonely man, reserved and aloof, and somewhat melancholy. His eldest son died very soon after he had left for New York — a tragedy Roberts seldom talked about, but which had been a cruel blow. Also, the unexpected death of his father in 1905 made it seem that a whole way of life had vanished forever.

Perhaps too, Roberts was disappointed in the turn his life had taken. He had exiled himself from the land he loved most, and his best writing, usually set in the New Brunswick of his childhood, is tinged with nostalgia and a sense of loss. Whatever was wrong, in his many travels Roberts seemed to be searching for something he could never find, and behind his witty conversation and brilliant social manner there was a deeper sadness.

Still, his career flourished. In 1903, he lectured in Toronto on Canadian literature — pointing out how few people realized that the man who was making nature stories popular, Ernest Thompson Seton, was a Canadian. The following year, the first of Roberts' own animal-story collections, *Kindred of the Wild*, appeared. There is a good preface to this book, in which Roberts surveyed the development of the animal story through the ages, and emphasized that realism and the psychology of the animal had become a leading concern. Animals and men both reason, but not necessarily in the same way. He ended by praising the animal story for offering readers escape from the workaday world, since such fiction allows us "to return to nature, without requiring that we at the same time return to barbarism."

In *Kindred of the Wild,* as in most of Roberts' animal-story collections, the theme is the conflict ever-present in nature. Roberts was especially interested in describing fights between animals over food or territory — following Darwin's idea that there is a continual struggle for survival in the natural world. Man is included in this struggle, and many stories measure the rights of animals against the assumptions of the human beings who hunt them.

Roberts was noted for describing the natural world in a more artistic manner than was expected for wilderness narratives. He never pretended to be a professional naturalist and he respected the scientific detail Seton was able to bring to his material. Several of Roberts' works are frankly unrealistic, such as *The Heart of the Ancient Wood,* which tells of a young girl who is brought up by a bear. She lives among the animals until she falls in love with a hunter; at the end her hunter is treed by the very bear that brought her up. The girl must face the dilemma of which one to save.

Dramatically it is a choice between nature and civilization. She chooses civilization by shooting the bear, but then blames her human lover for making her kill the wilderness mother. This is a far cry from the kind of work Seton was doing, but Seton admired Roberts' talent for meaningful fantasy. When a boy asked Seton, "Why don't you write something as good as *The Heart of the Ancient Wood*?" Seton answered, "I would if I could but I can't."

Most of Roberts' scientific facts are correct, however, and he had vivid memories of his own early experiences in the woods. When a friend told him it was a shame he was forced to write so many "beasties" to make a living, Roberts protested. "There's no shame about it. I'm just lucky that the kind of story I've always wanted to write should be fashionable today. All my recollections of animals and the wild country of my childhood were there just waiting to be written about."

But he had to endure an attack on the truth of his natural history, just as Seton did. In 1907, *Everybody's Magazine* in New York ran an article called "Roosevelt on the Nature Fakirs", in which the American President claimed that Roberts was a charming writer, but that most of his stories were really only fairy tales. Theodore Roosevelt, an amateur naturalist, was particularly disturbed by the fight between a lynx and some wolves described in Roberts' "On the Night Trail". Roberts replied that Roosevelt was thinking of the large Rocky Mountain animals, whereas he had written about the Canadian lynx and the small, eastern wolf.

The New York newspapers had a field day with the argument, and a parody of a typical animal story appeared in *The New York World* with comments supposedly added by Roosevelt ("TR") and Roberts ("CGDR"), which began this way:

It was night.
Bill, the trapper, saw two green orbs. He knew they were the eyes of a lynx caught in his steel trap.
TR: A mendacious mis-statement of fact. A lynx has not green eyes.
CGDR: This was a Canadian lynx; they are greener than the Manhattan kind.

Another paper published a cartoon about nature writers, Roberts, Seton, and Jack London included, holding toy animals and uttering preposterous facts of natural history, such as "Pigs make their nests in Chicago" and "Wolves will not eat scrambled eggs." The whole controversy was a friendly affair, little more than a joke, and Roberts and President Roosevelt became good friends after it had blown over.

By 1936, Roberts had published over two hundred nature stories. Perhaps his most well-known collections are *The Kindred of the Wild*, *The Haunters of the Silences*, and *Wisdom of the Wilderness*. Another good one, *Kings in Exile*, is about animals who are taken out of their natural habitat and are made into pets or put in zoos — a group of stories which has some bitter things to say about man's mistreatment of animals.

One of these stories is "The Summons of the North",

in which an orphaned polar-bear cub is shipped to a zoo. He seems indifferent to his fate until a blizzard reminds him of his lost Arctic home, and he dies from excitement and longing, sinking onto the floor of his man-made prison. Bears — more usually the black bear which inhabits the New Brunswick forest — were one of Roberts' favourite subjects. "The Monarch of Park Barren", also from *Kings in Exile*, describes an encounter between a bear and a magnificent moose which was driving all the other bulls off the Saugamauk ranges.

> The bear, as we have seen, was in no mood to give way. His small eyes glowed suddenly red with vengeful fury, as he wheeled and gathered himself, half crouching upon his haunches, to meet the tremendous attack. In this attitude all his vast strength was perfectly poised, ready for use in any direction. The moose, had he been attacking a rival of his own kind, would have charged with antlers down, but against all other enemies the weapons he relied upon were his gigantic hoofs, edged like chisels. As he reached his sullenly waiting antagonist he reared on his hind-legs, towering like a black rock about to fall and crush whatever was in its path. Like pile-drivers his fore-hoofs struck downwards, one closely following the other.
>
> The bear swung aside as lightly as a weasel, and eluded, but only by a hair's breadth, that destructive stroke. As he wheeled he delivered a terrific, swinging blow, with his armed forepaw, upon his assailant's shoulder.

There is also an excellent book-length biography along Seton lines, *Red Fox*, which describes the cunning and final triumph of a much-hunted animal.

Many of Roberts' animal books can be found with illustrations by the American artist Charles Livingston Bull, who was Roberts' own choice. Another Roberts illustrator was Paul Bransom.

These stories did not match the popularity of Seton's, but they sold well. So did Roberts' historical fiction, especially *Barbara Ladd*, an adventure set in the American Revolution. This novel was published in 1902, the same year as *The Kindred of the Wild*. Not many people read Roberts' historical romances any more, although they contain plenty of action, and have exciting — if somewhat preposterous — plots. Most of them, like *A Sister to Evangeline*, are set in Canada during the French and English conflicts of the eighteenth century. They come complete with noble, unhappy lovers (one French and the other English, naturally) and a horde of evil Indians, mad witches, plotting priests, exiled Acadians, and faithful backwoodsmen, all rushing about the forests bent on secret missions. Even these books have their origins in the Tantramar days, for Roberts used to play near the ruined French fort of Beauséjour on visits to an uncle, and hear the sad legends of Acadian history.

The historical romances are not Roberts at his best, but they made him money enough for living comfortably as he grew older. However, when World War I broke out in 1914, his patriotic zeal made it impossible for him to sit idly by while the troops were massing for action. Over-age at fifty-four, he was in such good health he didn't look it, so he boldly enlisted in the Frontiersmen, a squadron drawn from all over the British Empire.

He found to his relief that no one in the squadron was at all curious about his age. When he made friends with a man who looked about fifty himself, he couldn't help confessing the secret: "Don't tell a soul, but I'm fifty-four."

The other man looked very serious, and then peered around to see if anyone was listening.

"I'll keep your secret if you'll keep mine. I'm *seventy*. I just couldn't stay out of the fight, though."

"I guess there's a place for experience in wartime, as well as youth," Roberts said, laughing.

"Quite so. You know, I hear there's a shortage of the more mature officers at the front. Why not apply for a commission? The Germans are killing off our British officers like rabbits."

This was not much of an advertisement for officer-training, but Roberts thought it over, and eventually applied. He did not, however, fill in the blank on the forms concerning his date of birth, and added a little note saying he would have lied about it, but his birthdate was there for anybody to see in *Who's Who* and the *Encyclopaedia Britannica*.

His English friends were horrified.

"You can't make jokes like that with our War Office!" said one. "Now you'll be turned down."

His acceptance came back with the date filled in as 1870 — making him ten years younger than he really was — and there was also a note from the War Office: "Some rascal has been taking liberties with the date of your birth but you can settle with him for the perjury when the war is over."

On another form, however, Roberts gave the true

dates for his marriage and the births of his children. When he was called before the War Office for posting, he noticed with horror that the General had both forms before him.

"Well, Mr Roberts," the General said drily, "you Canadians are a precocious lot. Married at ten years of age, I see."

Roberts did not dare to speak and the General glanced down at the papers again.

"And your first child when you were only twelve. A most happy event, I'm sure."

Then to Roberts' relief, the General smiled.

"I should judge, Mr Roberts, that if your past history is any indication, you will make a most efficient officer."

In 1916, Major Roberts was sent to France as Special Press Correspondent attached to the Canadian Corps. He spent much time at the front writing articles on the battles. Conditions were crude, with the noise of artillery booming away and the calls of the soldiers mocking the enemy's aim as shells just missed the dugout. In 1918, Roberts was called back to London to work with Lord Beaverbrook on an official history of the war *(Canada in Flanders)*, and was on hand for the wild celebration in Trafalgar Square when the armistice was declared.

After this, he settled down in London, soon publishing more volumes of animal stories. Also, in 1919 came *In the Morning of Time*, an adventure set in prehistoric times, which shows man evolving into a civilized being while beset by earthquakes, giant dragonflies, and woolly mammoths. He continued his travels, adding the Channel Islands and North Africa to his list of places visited. But increasingly his thoughts were turning toward Canada. His daughter Edith visited him in London in 1922 and urged him to come home with her. The next year his sister, and then his mother, passed away, and soon his son Douglas had crossed the Atlantic in the hope that he could convince his father to return.

"By nature, I am a wanderer," Roberts would say to these entreaties, but his homeland had never been far from his mind during the long years abroad. From his writing, it is clear that in his imagination he still lived in Canada as much as possible. For example, while touring the desert towns of North Africa, he wrote a story about the life of a New Brunswick snowshoe rabbit, "The Little Homeless One" — describing perfectly the cool woodland scenery he had not explored in over a quarter of a century.

At last the news that Bliss Carman was making a highly successful series of lecture tours across Canada whetted Roberts' interest in going back. On February 5, 1925, he returned to give a reading in Toronto, and scored a great personal triumph. The newspapers welcomed the homecoming of a famous native writer, and his role as a pioneer of the country's literature was confirmed by references to him as "Father of Canadian Poetry".

In the busy years that followed, Roberts criss-crossed Canada many times, reading and lecturing in towns from Halifax to Victoria. He was a popular speaker, never at a loss for words when things went wrong. In Trail, British Columbia, one night, he fell backwards off the improvised platform, and recovered himself with

"That was just to illustrate how rapidly the wild creatures can disappear on occasion." And once, while reading an animal story in Orillia, Ontario, he noticed a large Newfoundland dog amble into the lecture hall, sit at the end of the front row, and regard him with sad, soulful eyes. Roberts paused and said to the dog: "Thank you, Old Chap, for your mark of approval, testifying to the fact that I know animals."

Everywhere he was greeted by admirers, not all of them human beings. In Vancouver, a flock of seagulls began visiting his hotel window, screaming wildly and flocking to the ledge where Roberts would give them scraps of toast and bacon. One ancient gull, bigger and more aristocratic than the rest, always refused to scramble for his food. Perched on one side of the window, he waited until the rabble had finished, and then allowed Roberts to feed him porridge from a large spoon.

Honours and awards seemed to follow him wherever he went. He was the first person to receive the Lorne Pierce Medal for Canadian Literature. This was in 1926, and in 1927 he was elected national president of the Canadian Authors' Association. The Sarcee Indians placed a warbonnet on his head in Calgary in 1928, renaming him Na-Kee-Tlee-Se Ah-Kee-Tcha, or Chief Great Scribe. Chief Joe Big Plume, an admirer of Roberts' nature stories, explained the reason for the honour: "We want one of our own, one who knows us, who knows our life and the life of the wilderness."

The year 1935 brought another, less tongue-twisting honorary title, when Roberts was knighted by King George V. It was now *Sir* Charles.

But these later years were also marked with pain. His

companion, cousin, and fellow poet, Bliss Carman, died in 1929, and he saw many other old friends go to their rest: these great sorrows were an inevitable part of a long life. In 1938, he made a sentimental journey to the Tantramar country he had so often celebrated. The parsonage had burned down, but his father's church was still there, and he played a hymn on the reedy, old organ in the choir-loft. The long sweep of marshland and bay had not changed, but some of the woods where he had climbed trees and collected birds' eggs had been cleared for farms. Things were not the same, but he had never expected time to stand still for him, preserving the land of his childhood exactly as he remembered it. Walking through the fields, he sniffed the sea-air while some lines from "Tantramar Revisited" ran through his head:

> Ah the old-time stir, how once it stung me with rapture —
> Old-time sweetness, the winds freighted with honey and salt!

Old-time sweetness....His career had been brilliant; he had travelled widely, met many people, and done many things. But perhaps nothing had ever matched the happiness of those early years on the Tantramar.

Knowing the past could not be recaptured, Roberts settled in Toronto, where he lived well into his eighties. During World War II, he accepted the fact that this time he was a bit too old for combat, but he made his contribution with vigorous patriotic poems and essays. Several months before his death, he married Joan

Montgomery and saw the publication of a long, enthusiastic biography of himself by Elsie M. Pomeroy. He died on November 26, 1943, and his body was returned to New Brunswick for burial.

Roberts will always be important as the Father of Canadian Poetry, and some people are surprised to find that he wrote animal stories at all. But in the stories, his deep feeling for the Canadian land is expressed as much as in his most resounding patriotic poem. A Maritimer never forgets, and throughout his active and restless life Roberts was always true to his early education in the ways of nature and to the familiar marshes and woodlands of his New Brunswick home.

# Grey Owl

In April 1938, newspaper readers were startled by headlines which crowded even Adolf Hitler off the front pages:

FAMED INDIAN REALLY A WHITE MAN!
Friend of the Beaver Exposed!
GREY OWL A FRAUD!

Studying the photo of the popular writer who had died only a few days before, many people could not believe what they read. The picture showed a lean, hawk-nosed man in buckskins, the very image of an Indian chieftain. There was a feather in his black, braided hair, and he faced the world with the dignified gaze of a wise, old warrior. Could this man be from a respectable British family? It seemed impossible.

It was true that his eyes were not brown like an Indian's, but pale blue. His champions insisted that Grey Owl had never claimed to be more than a halfbreed, the son of a Scottish father and an Apache woman named Katherine Cochise. However, during the height of his fame, the press had gone out of its way to label him a "full-blooded" Indian and he had done nothing to correct the false impression. People who had been profoundly moved by Grey Owl's lectures on the wilderness now felt they had been taken in, and sales of his books began to drop off.

Admirers of the man's conservation work, particularly his efforts to save the beaver from extinction, thought the newspapers were trying to discredit a hero, and bitter controversy broke out. But as more details came to light, it could not be denied that the man who called himself Wa-Sha-Quon-Asin, or Grey Owl, was born Archibald Stansfield Belaney in 1888, and had been brought up in comfortable surroundings in Hastings, England.

The controversy simmered down as World War II began to occupy everyone's mind. Even today, with the renewed interest in Grey Owl's life and work, there are many mysteries which remain unsolved. The facts that are known, however, make his biography a good example of the old saying that "truth is stranger than fiction."

Hastings has long been a quiet, seaside town with a large population of widows and retired army personnel. One August afternoon in the 1890's, a pretty, anxious-looking woman knocked at the door of one of the best homes in town. She was Katherine Cox Belaney, on a visit to her son, Archie, who lived here with his aunts and grandmother. Katherine had two younger children to look after, and was able to see Archie only when the ladies permitted. Her husband, George Belaney, was somewhere in America. He was the black sheep of the Belaney family, and had been given an allowance on the understanding that he would not return to England.

Katherine had remained here with her children, dependent on her husband's relatives for money. It was a hard, threadbare life she led, and lifting the fancy brass door-knocker again, she could not help sighing. If only George had not been so wild, she might be living in this grand house herself, instead of just visiting as a poor relation.

At last a servant opened the door and Katherine was ushered into the hall. It was silent as a church, and the polished clock and shelves of china gleamed richly in the semi-darkness. Tea, she was informed would be late, so she decided to go upstairs and see Archie. As she mounted the staircase, she could not help thinking of her husband....

The scandal had rocked all Hastings when George had married her sister Elizabeth, the daughter of a tavern keeper. Katherine had gone with the married couple to Florida, where the older Mrs Belaney had bought her son an orange grove. She had hoped that marriage, even such a disgraceful one, would turn him into a hard-working, sober citizen.

Seldom sober, never hard-working, George soon let the orange grove run to ruin, and when her sister had died, he had proposed to Katherine, who was thirteen years old at the time. Katherine had accepted, and in due course was pregnant with Archie. They returned to England for the birth, George clearly hoping that his mother would shell out more money at the prospect of a Belaney grandson.

With a shudder, Katherine recalled their homecoming, and the horrified looks she had got from the Belaney ladies, particularly Aunt Ada. Of course, George had botched everything from the start, bracing himself up with a bottle of scotch the first night back. Well, wherever he was, she could guess what he was doing. Drinking, no doubt, and probably with some low kind of woman. But perhaps he was alone, and was thinking of her and the children....

Lost in thought, she barely noticed something flow like quicksilver along the step where she was about to place her foot. Then she drew back in terror and screamed.

There on the carpet was a long, grey snake with

brown markings. Katherine clung to the banister and screamed again.

"Mercy sakes, Kitty, what is it?"

Aunt Ada and Aunt Carrie appeared at the bottom of the stairs, and behind them was the small, upright figure of her mother-in-law, Mrs Belaney.

Speechless with fear, Katherine could only point to the monster at her feet.

"Don't be a fool, Kitty. It's only Rajah," Aunt Ada said with a sniff. "You know, one of Archie's snakes, from his menagerie in the attic."

"Don't worry, my dear. It's harmless," gently added Aunt Carrie. "Archie removed the fangs, so it can't bite."

Katherine dared to look down at the snake, which was coiling in the corner, its forked tongue darting swiftly in and out. It seemed frightened too.

Suddenly a slender, dark-eyed boy rushed down the steps, his cheeks flushed.

"Mother, did you hurt him? Poor Rajah." He kneeled down, and holding the snake's head close to his own, began stroking it.

Katherine screamed again.

"Katherine, stop that! What will the neighbours think?" said Aunt Ada. "Rajah's all right, Archie. Your mother didn't know he was a pet, and was a trifle...surprised. I must say these animals of yours are getting to be a nuisance. Now get Rajah back upstairs, and Katherine you come into the drawing room. You'd think we were living in a circus!"

After a few cups of tea, Katherine had recovered enough to ask, "Is he allowed to keep animals in the house?"

"Allowed!" exclaimed Grandmother Belaney. "Try and stop that boy when he has his mind set on something! And he's crazy about nature, just like his poor father. It's a bad sign."

Katherine looked at the glass case in the corner which held a stuffed weasel attacking a stuffed hare. George had been interested in taxidermy long ago, and examples of his work were all over the house. "There's nothing wrong with nature study," she said timidly. "And Archie is interested in live animals, not stuffed ones. I should think that was a good sign."

"Oh yes, much healthier," said Aunt Carrie brightly, but Grandmother Belaney only frowned at her teacup, and Aunt Ada gave a refined snort.

"He's much more serious and hard-working than George, too," Aunt Carrie continued recklessly, trying to be helpful. "Poor George. Our brother was just too easy-going. To think of all his talents thrown away like that. If only he hadn't been so restless. Why I remember when he was seeing that barmaid at the Star and Crown...."

"Carrie!" warned Aunt Ada. "There are things we do *not* talk about at the tea-table."

Katherine stood up abruptly. Her sister Elizabeth had been "that barmaid", and all this talk about George, as if he were a dead man, made her blood boil. But she couldn't risk offending these ladies, so she smiled weakly and said: "I'm going up to see Archie and meet his animals. After all, I don't want to step on anything else while I'm here."

In the room at the top of the house, Archie was delighted to show her the other snakes, the frogs, the swallow with the broken wing, and his prize possession, a baby rabbit he had found by the side of its dead mother. The rabbit was just learning to trust Archie and it responded shyly to his calls and caresses. Katherine watched her son as he was absorbed in his pets. His dark good looks and the intensity in his eyes reminded her of somebody.

"My, but you're starting to look like your father," she said.

Archie set the rabbit down immediately. "Tell me about him," he demanded. "They won't say anything about him here. Is he a brave man? Has he gone to Canada to live with the Indians? Do I really take after him?"

Katherine was uncomfortable: she had not meant to bring the subject up at all. The boy's excitement disturbed her. His health was good, but he was growing up to be high-strung and nervous. It couldn't be good for him to be in a household with so many women and no men.

"If I talk about your father, will you promise to keep it a secret from...them?" she asked.

"I swear it."

This solemn response made Katherine more uneasy than ever. She knew well that the subject was a forbidden one, but she had never before seen Archie so interested in anything she had to say.

"He's a fine man," she said finally. "A true hero of the outdoors. He was a great friend of Buffalo Bill's. Did you know that?"

"Did he ever live with the Indians?"

"Yes, of course. I remember him telling me once about an experience he had with the Apaches...."

Katherine's imagination expanded with the eager, blazing attention of her son, and she found herself telling some stories that strayed far from the truth. It was getting dark in the room when the servant came up to announce dinner, but she could still see the ecstatic look on Archie's face as he turned to her and announced: "When I grow up I am going to join my father and live with the Indians."

Then he left the room. Katherine tried to smile at his childish enthusiasm, but there was something about it which impressed and worried her. Perhaps she shouldn't be filling his head with these tales, but what harm could it do? She went to the window and looked out over the Belaney estate, well tended by the gardener, and now deep in purplish shadow as the sun set. At least she could give her son a hero for a father, even if she couldn't afford a fine house or a proper family life.

Actually, Archie did not seem very taken with the fine house or the other advantages of living with the Belaney ladies. He spent much of his time outside, taking solitary walks along the sea-coast. His aunts were worried about this at first, and grew irritated by his habit of saying "Nothing" every time they asked what he'd been doing all day. Punishments and restrictions were of no use, for Archie had a way of vanishing when their backs were turned. He was never a disobedient child, but when he wanted his own way, he would try to get it with a silent persistence that usually won out over all protests.

He had a good reason for taking long walks, and that reason was Aunt Ada. Determined to make her nephew a gentleman if it killed him, she decided to educate the boy at home until he was ten, so he wouldn't be warped by "bad influences". She was after him all day, fidgeting with his clothes, counting time when he played the piano, correcting his grammar, and watching like a hawk to see that he used the right fork at meals. Archie was a natural southpaw. Ada saw this as a crime against Queen and country, and whenever he would use his left hand, there would be a whack on the knuckles from the wooden pointer she carried.

But even Aunt Ada grew concerned about his isolation from other boys, and all the Belaney ladies had high hopes that he would make friends when he entered the Hastings Grammar School in 1899. When he came home from school in the evenings, they were so eager to hear about the other boys, that he obligingly began to invent stories about what had happened to himself and his "chums". The ladies were delighted.

"We must have all your friends to tea," Aunt Ada said one day. "I have the school list of addresses right here, and I'll send out the invitations tonight."

Embarrassed, Archie tried to stall her off, but she was determined. Finally he had to confess that he had made it all up to please them, since they seemed so interested in what was for him a dull round of classes and organized games. Aunt Ada was more puzzled than angry. Archie was athletic, good-looking, and not in the least shy. Why wasn't he making himself popular at school?

The reason was simple. Archie wasn't interested in popularity, and the other boys' chatter about cricket and rugby struck him as a waste of time. And his classmates thought this tall, silent boy, with his passion for Indians and western books, rather peculiar. During lunch hour, one of the top boys in the school once came upon Archie lying flat on his stomach in the grass.

"I say there, Belaney, what are you doing down there? Catching worms?"

Archie frowned, made a motion for the boy to be quiet, and returned to his prone position.

"Come now, Belaney, this is too bad of you. What game is it?"

"It's no game. I'm learning to be an Indian," Archie said, trying to sound as friendly as he could.

"Now that's jolly." The boy patted his mouth in a war-whoop. "Indians are lots of fun. I'll call the others, and we can play robbing a wagon train or burning down the fort."

"I'm trying to creep up on that sundial without breaking a twig or rustling the grass. That's what real Indians do."

"Oh. How long does that take?"

"At least an hour. Do you want to try it?" Archie added politely.

"It does take a frightfully long time, doesn't it?" said the boy, eyeing the sundial with distrust. "No, I really don't think I will, you know."

Relieved that the interruption was over, Archie returned to his self-discipline and the boy went back to tell his friends what an odd bird that Belaney was, stalking a sundial on his hands and knees. But Archie didn't mind what the others thought. He did well in school — preparing his lessons carefully but without much enthusiasm. His aunts fussed about his silences and his interest in Indians, but on the whole he seemed a happy, ordinary boy, although the faraway look in his eye might have warned them that he was not going to settle down in Hastings and go into business as they assumed he would.

For in Archie's mind a grand plan was taking shape. This had to do with vast wildernesses and cold, blue lakes disturbed only by the silent wake of a birchbark canoe. Overhead an arrow of geese flew south in the pale sunset, and sitting by a campfire, dressed in furs and Indian robes, was the figure of a magnificent hunter — his father. This was the world Archie really inhabited as he went through the daily motions of attending classes and pouring tea for the ladies.

One day he came home to find that the ladies had a visitor, and what was more important, the visitor had a beautiful daughter in her early teens, just his age.

"Archie, please take Ivy up and show her the animals. I'm sure she's desperately bored listening to our gossip."

At the top of the house, Archie displayed his precious collection. Now he had several hutches filled with rabbits, as well as some silkworms, and a handsome weasel which snarled at everyone else, but allowed Archie to scratch it behind the ears like a kitten. Florence Ivy Holmes admired everything, although she was wary of Rajah. Suddenly Archie had an impulse to tell her his plan.

"When I leave school in a few years, I am going to Canada."

"To fight the Indians?" asked Ivy.

"No, to *be* an Indian. First I will find my father, who

has been adopted by an Indian tribe and is helping the red man to regain his rights."

Ivy, who had heard very different stories about what Archie's father was doing in America, wisely said nothing. She studied the dark-complexioned youth in his school collar and tie, and decided that he was quite good-looking.

"You're dark enough to pass for an Indian yourself," she said. "Have you told your aunts and grandmother about this plan?"

"No, but I will in my last year of school."

"I'm sure they'll be disappointed," Ivy said. "They could get you a fine job here in England."

"England! Who wants to live in dumb, boring England?" Archie exclaimed, a flush reddening his lean face. "You won't catch me wearing a stupid collar and tie all my life. I'm going to wear real deerskin and live with Indians in the woods and learn their language!"

At this outburst, the weasel growled and the rabbits rustled in their cages. In spite of herself, Ivy was more impressed with Archie than ever; none of the other boys she knew had an ounce of spirit compared with this one. She decided to get her mother to visit the Belaney ladies more often.

As time passed, Archie read more about the Indians, and on fine nights, would slide down the drain-pipe and creep around the house like an enemy scout. He played Indian constantly at school, called himself Big Chief, and even tried to convince his schoolmates that he had Indian blood. When only a few months of school remained, he announced his plan to go to Canada after graduation. He had expected opposition, but was unprepared for the flurry of protest from the Belaney ladies.

"You're only sixteen," said Grandmother Belaney gravely. "It's too serious a step for someone so young."

"Oh please don't go, Archie!" cried Aunt Carrie. "We'd miss you so! Wouldn't we miss him, Ada?"

"Your father threw his life away over there," Aunt Ada snapped. "And now you, with all your schooling and advantages, want to do the same. Well, we won't permit it!"

It was a stormy April in the Belaney household. While Archie studied for his final examinations, the ladies secretly set to work finding him a job that would appeal to his love of the outdoors. At last they settled on a position with a surveying company, but Archie would have none of it.

"I won't. You might as well condemn me to a jail cell. I know the kind of life I want!"

Somehow, after a summer of arguments and tears, a compromise was struck. Archie agreed to work for the surveyors for six months. If after that time he didn't want to continue, or if the company was not satisfied with his performance, the ladies would pay his passage to Canada. However, if he left, he was never to expect another penny from them.

During the next six months, Archie worked with his usual patience and intelligence, and his boss was delighted with him. The aunts and Grandmother Belaney watched Archie carefully for any signs of excitement over his new job, or any hint that his crazy dream of the Canadian woods was losing its hold. He went about his business happily enough, but there was still that faraway look in his eyes. He seemed to be waiting for something, marking time.

When the six months were up, he went into the drawing room where the ladies were having tea. Looking at the kindly, worried faces of Grandmother Belaney and Aunt Carrie, he felt a surge of affection for these women who had raised him as best they knew how. A glance at Aunt Ada, however, strengthened his resolve to say what he had to say: "I have given the company notice of my resignation, and sold Rajah and the rabbits. Tomorrow, I'll let the weasel loose in the woods. Then it will be time for me to leave for Canada."

Defeated, as usual, by his persistence, the ladies gave in, and made him a present of a new suit along with his ticket across the Atlantic.

"Oh Ada," said Aunt Carrie with tears in her eyes, as they watched the ship leave the harbour, "the house is going to seem so empty with Archie gone. I do hope he'll be all right over there."

"Like father, like son," Aunt Ada remarked grimly.

For his part, Archie was overjoyed to be free of England at last. Day after day he paced the deck in the freezing winds as the other passengers stayed warm inside. He would need to toughen up if he expected to go north right away. He was booked for Halifax, but a man on board convinced him to continue to Toronto and work for awhile, especially after finding out how much money Archie had brought with him.

"Five pounds! But that's less than twenty-five dollars! You won't last long in Canada on that amount, I can tell you."

Archie had the sense to realize that he would have to

postpone his dream for a bit longer, and soon he was hanging up men's jackets and measuring trouser seams in a dreary shop on King Street. Toronto was not his idea of Canada at all, with its streetcars, concrete, and scurrying crowds of people. None of the pale young men he worked with were interested in anything but money, and they thought he was daft because he studied maps instead of joining them at the pool hall after work. Nobody he met seemed aware of the mighty wilderness that stretched away to the north of the city.

Archie tried to save money, but rent and meals in greasy restaurants swallowed up most of his salary. As the days crawled by, he began to worry. Had he come all this way only to waste his life in a city?

It was 1906, and there had been another silver strike at Cobalt. Once news reached Toronto of the fortunes to be made, everybody was talking about the northern wilderness. Archie wasn't much interested in mining silver, but he thought the rush north would mean some odd jobs opening up in the area. Scraping his savings together, he had just enough for train fare to Latchford, a small settlement south of Cobalt. It would not be easy, but anything was better than rotting in Toronto.

As the train chugged out of Union Station, Archie noticed that one of the other passengers — a dark, ugly, weatherbeaten man — was watching him.

"Excuse me, sir," Archie said shyly. "Would you be going as far as Cobalt?"

"Could be," was the short reply. "Reckon you ain't, though."

"What do you mean?"

"Them clothes for one thing. That fancy accent of yours for another."

Archie blushed, although he told himself there was no reason to be ashamed. He knew the blue suit his aunts had given him was no good for the bush, but he didn't have any other clothes. And as for his upper-class British drawl, all the Canadians made fun of it, even though he tried hard to imitate their flat, harsh-sounding accent.

"I'd stay out of the north if I was you, kid," said the ugly man, sauntering away down the aisle. "It's a dirty place for a greenhorn."

A greenhorn! Well, the man was right. Reading and dreaming about the outdoors were no substitute for actual experience in the woods, and for a brief moment Archie began to wonder if the whole trip wasn't a mistake. But as the landscape outside his window changed from cultivated farmland to scrub forest and pink granite, his spirits revived. The north was where he belonged. He had always known that, and it would take more than a passing stranger's insults to keep him away.

Seven miles from his destination, there was a washout on the tracks and the passengers were told bluntly that they could walk from here. Archie reached Latchford in a state of exhaustion, his blue suit torn and mud-stained. He soon found that there were no jobs for an unskilled man in the town, and he was not the type to make new friends easily or to beg on the streets. Flat broke by this time, he slept on the bare ground and ate nothing at all. One evening he got into a fight with a man who was trying to steal his blue jacket, and a bystander took pity on him.

"Come over here, lad, and have some stew. And let's try to get you some real clothes. That outfit of yours makes you stick out like a sore thumb."

Archie gratefully accepted the worn overalls and flannel shirt, although he didn't say much about it since people seemed to get suspicious whenever they heard his accent. The next day he decided to walk the forty-five miles to Cobalt and make a fresh start looking for work. It was a damp, hot day in the height of the black-fly season, and the stew in his stomach seemed to have turned to battery acid. He could not stop himself from scratching at the insect bites, and after a few miles of trudging along the railway tracks a cold sweat broke out all over his body.

Soon he was delirious with fever and did not hear the train roaring up behind him. He jumped out of the way just in time, but long after the caboose had passed, he still lay where he had fallen. His muscles seemed to have dissolved and the sky was whirling about overhead. Before he blanked out completely, he realized that the flies were settling in swarms on his face and arms.

When he opened his eyes again, he was looking straight into the ugly face of the man who had called him a greenhorn on the train. Behind him were two Indians, and behind them the rough wall of a log cabin. "I'm either dreaming or crazy," Archie thought.

"Well, kid, I reckon you'll be all right," said the ugly man. "Lucky we come across you when we did, or you'd be food for the wolves by now."

"You...the train...," Archie said, but he was too weak to say more.

The man gave a broad grin. "Yep, it's me, and I recognize you too. Don't worry, I ain't always so mean as I was on the train. When I go into town I get drunk, and that makes me ornery. But out here in the bush, I reckon I'm O.K."

The man said his name was Jesse Hood, a professional guide in the summer, a trapper in winter, and a hard drinker in the fall and spring. "It's sort of my natural pattern," he explained. "I'd feel funny if I did it any different."

Archie looked beyond Jesse and tried to bring the two Indians into focus. One was an old man in a headdress of fur and feathers, who crouched by a steaming, fragrant kettle and tapped rhythmically on a drum.

"That's Ag-Nu," Jesse said. "No doctors up here in Temagami. Medicine man's better anyway. That stuff he's brewing will fix you up in no time, you can bet. And the girl is Angele."

Angele was slender and lovely, and she giggled flirtatiously when she realized that Archie was looking at her. "It's a dream," Archie thought, "or I've died and gone to heaven."

Ag-Nu's medicine and Angele's presence soon had Archie on his feet again, and reluctantly he began planning to move on. But Jesse was going out on a trip for the Government in a few weeks, and after he heard Archie's story, offered to hire him as a packer if he could learn to handle a canoe by then. Michelle, a young Ojibway Indian and an expert woodsman, would be his instructor, if Archie was willing.

Was Archie willing! The next weeks were like a dream come true, with an Indian teaching him the fine art of long-distance canoeing on a beautiful northern lake surrounded by pine forest. Archie was awed by Michelle's knowledge and strength, and Michelle, pleased by his pupil's admiration, soon became a close friend. However, aching muscles and a stiff back proved that it was no dream. After a day of hard paddling, he would drop into bed so bone-weary that he knew he would never rise again. By the end of the two weeks he had learned enough to satisfy Jesse Hood.

The summer-long canoe trip, with its many portages and storms, was Archie's great test of endurance in the wild. He had recently been ill, he was not used to hard physical labour, and although nobody realized this, he was seventeen years old. There were days when he thought his arms would drop off if he had to lift the paddle one more time, but somehow he persevered, and never uttered a word of complaint. He passed the test with flying colours, and at the end of the trip Jesse shook his hand and paid him a rare compliment: "I reckon you're all right, Belaney."

When autumn came, Jesse left for North Bay to get drunk, and Archie and Michelle settled down for the winter in a wilderness shack, where the Indian taught him trapping, snowshoeing and the Ojibway language. When Jesse did not return in the spring, Michelle decided to rejoin his people, and suggested that Archie try for work in Timiskaming area, which was just opening up for sportsmen and tourists.

Bill Guppy, who ran a resort on Lake Timiskaming, was surprised that the dark young man in buckskins should ask for a job in such a refined English accent. He was even more puzzled when he saw that the man he had hired preferred the company of the Ojibways to that of his own race. But Belaney worked hard and was a top-notch guide; white men and Indians alike were impressed by his quiet, unassuming manner and his proficiency in the bush. He never spoke about his past, but in the northern woods there were many men whose lives didn't bear a close examination, and people learned not to ask questions.

When Bill Guppy moved his operation to Lake Temagami, he took Archie with him, and to make sure his best guide didn't wander off during the winter, got him a job carrying the mail by dog sled. Archie spent three years with Mr Guppy and the Canadian postal service — thriving on the hearty outdoor life as if he had been born and bred to it. But it was not all work, for he had renewed his acquaintance with Angele.

Archie thought he was in love with the beautiful Ojibway, and was eager to get married. Her tribe was suspicious of this white man's interest in an Indian girl, although Archie had become a familiar figure at Bear Island. In fact, with his deerskins and tan, and his command of the Ojibway language, it was hard to distinguish him from the Indians there. His white friends warned him that Angele had a reputation for being wild, but Archie wouldn't listen to anybody, and he married her quietly in 1910.

The Bear Island people struck Angele's name off the tribal role, and Archie's other friends shook their heads sadly at the news. Furious at such opposition, Archie persuaded Angele to come away with him to the south of Lake Temagami, where he set up as a trapper.

It was a gloomy winter. After so much fuss, Archie found that married life didn't suit him, and the homesick Angele was often left alone in the cabin for weeks while he was away trapping. She gave birth to a daughter in the spring, and the next day Archie left to go hunting. He returned in the late fall for a month's visit, then abandoned both the mother and child, and moved westward to Biscotasing, in the Algoma district. Angele returned to Bear Island, where everyone said "I told you so," tried to decide whose fault it was, and then forgot the whole thing.

For the next three winters, Archie followed the rough and lonely trade of the fur trapper. He fought forest fires for the Government in the summers, and nobody questioned the fact that he belonged to the Indian Section of Fire Rangers. His accent had all but vanished, his face was brown from the sun and wind, and he wore his black hair in plaits. He never mentioned England, and during his years in Canada he had sent the ladies in Hastings exactly one postcard — and that had been during the first weeks in Toronto.

Archie was fighting fires when the news reached Ontario about the war in Europe. Hardly anyone in the bush knew what it was all about, but many immediately hitched rides to the nearest towns to enlist, Archie among them. The horrors of the so-called "Great War" were a shock to everyone, but especially to the Canadian "half-breed", as Archie identified himself in his army documents, who had been so long away from civilization. The senseless killing disgusted him and he withdrew into himself, as he had long ago with his schoolmates, speaking only when spoken to and making no friends among the men in his unit.

In 1917, he was wounded in the foot, and his lungs

were seared by mustard gas which he had inhaled. Sent to an English hospital to recuperate, he wondered if he would ever be strong enough to return to the wilderness. Brooding over the war in his hospital bed, he began to believe that this was the end of the white man's civilization. The white man had always been evil and violent; he had done his best to destroy the Indian and the natural world, and now he was bent on destroying himself. Archie felt he had been a fool to become involved in this white man's war, but soon he would escape back to the woods and his own people.

These feverish thoughts were interrupted one day when the nurse announced that he had visitors. Somehow the Belaney ladies had discovered his whereabouts.

"Can you imagine, Archie? The receptionist told me you were an Indian from Ontario." Aunt Ada adjusted her glasses and peered more closely at the patient. "Archie, that *is* you, isn't it?"

"Of course it's Archie," Aunt Carrie insisted. "And the doctors say you're well enough to come with us now. We're taking you home."

Home. As he sat with his foot propped up on an overstuffed footstool in the drawing room at Hastings, Archie realized that this had never been home for him, although by some accident he had grown up here. His home was a larger place, with forests and icy lakes, not this stuffy little house. He inhaled deeply, trying to get a breath of fresh air, and there was a sharp stab of pain in his lungs. Perhaps he would never be well again, he thought grimly. And they said that mustard gas affected the brain: perhaps that was why he had been so depressed. Oh, this white man's civilization, how he hated it!

In the midst of his depression at Hastings, Ivy Holmes appeared like an angel from heaven. Long ago he had taken her upstairs to see his animals and had told her about his plans for Canada. Now she had grown into a beautiful woman, eager to hear about the life he'd been leading in the north, unlike his aunts who never mentioned the subject. With Ivy around, his health improved and he began to make plans to show her the country she seemed so interested in hearing about.

They were married in February, just before Archie went up to London to have his health checked. To his surprise, he was declared unfit for further active service, awarded a pension, and discharged from the Army. Ivy, naturally, was overjoyed by the turn of events.

"Now we can settle down, and you can find a job in Hastings," she said, running her fingers through his black hair. "Of course, you'll need to go to the barber first. You're looking like a regular savage."

Archie laughed. "I always wear it this way in Canada. Don't you see? Now I can take you back there."

"Canada? Well, certainly I'd like to visit the country some day, but...."

"I don't mean just to visit. We'll build our own cabin in the woods, and I'll teach you how to paddle a canoe."

"Oh Archie, surely you don't expect *me* to...."

Soon he realized the truth: Ivy had no intention of leaving England. Archie felt that he had been tricked. Like every member of this corrupt, white civilization, she was a hypocrite and a cheat. Angrily he twisted the

## WITH US AGAIN WITH WONDERFUL FILMS!

After a brilliant and overwhelmingly successful tour

of

The British Isles and the United States

and

A Command Performance at Buckingham Palace

# GREY OWL

WILL SHOW HIS PICTURES AND TALK ON

### "BACK TO MY BEAVER PEOPLE"
— AT —

### MASSEY HALL, SATURDAY, MARCH 26th

Commencing 8 p.m. sharp. Doors open 7.30.

**RESERVE YOUR SEATS EARLY AND BRING YOUR FRIENDS!**

Tickets: $1.00 and 50c.

Remember! If you want your seats in blocks book early!
Tickets may be secured by telephoning Mr. Eric Gaskell, RA. 2867, or Mrs. King, HU. 1441.

### THE STUDENT'S IMPRESSION OF GREY OWL!

The Toronto Branch of The Canadian Authors' Association offers two prizes for the best essays by any high or secondary school student on the theme of Grey Owl's appearance and remarks while on the Massey Hall platform on the evening of March 26th.

#### *FIRST PRIZE!*
ANY TWO OF GREY OWL'S BOOKS (AUTOGRAPHED)

"Tales of an Empty Cabin"   "Sajo and Her Beaver People"   "Pilgrims of the Wild"
"Men of the Last Frontier"   "The Tree"

#### *SECOND PRIZE!*
ANY ONE OF THE FIVE

Preferred length 300 words. Limit 500 words. Entries to reach Mr. Eric Gaskell, 40 Nanton Ave., Toronto, by April 9th. Presentations will be made at the Canadian Authors' Association Annual Dinner May 14th.

UNDER THE AUSPICES OF THE TORONTO BRANCH
OF THE CANADIAN AUTHOR'S ASSOCIATION

*1938*

*Grey Owl at Niagara Falls, 1937*

*Grey Owl and Jelly Roll*

*Anahareo with Sir Charles G. D. Roberts at Riding Mountain National Park, 1931*

new wedding ring from his finger and flung it to the carpet. Let all Europe go up in flames — he was going home!

When Archie returned to northern Ontario, it is possible that his bitterness drove him slightly crazy. He would rave on about the evil white man, the slaughter he had witnessed at the front, and the spreading terror of a war which he didn't seem to understand was now over. He flared up at friends and strangers alike, and soon got a reputation for bad temper. Nobody would hire such a man as a guide, and this fed his supicions about white society even more. He ignored his weakened foot and limped through the woods like a wild animal in all weathers — forgetting to feed himself or to keep warm. If some of the Indians had not watched over him, he probably would have died.

Rejecting civilization altogether, he lived with an Ojibway tribe; he spoke the language of the Ojibways and followed their ways completely. He had never found his real father, but during these years he had a substitute father in a magnificent, old Indian called Neganikabu ("He Who Stands First"), who trained him in the Ojibway manhood rituals. One proud night, as the others chanted around a huge bonfire, Neganikabu bestowed upon Archie his new name, to signify that he had been officially adopted by the tribe. He was no longer Archibald Belaney, but Wa-Sha-Quon-Asin: literally, "Shining Beak", or Grey Owl.

It was as if he had been born again. Secure in his new identity as an Indian, his attitude toward the white world changed from hatred to indifference. His physical strength was restored as he steadily regained his usual modesty, humour, and self-control. Soon he had won back his former reputation as a responsible tourist guide and was no longer regarded with pity and contempt as the wild man of the woods.

The years passed uneventfully until one summer in 1925, when he was working as a guide for a Temagami resort. He noticed a young Indian girl edging away from a group of rowdy white men.

"Don't worry about them," he told her. "Whites aren't any more dangerous than most of us."

She turned and smiled mischievously as she noticed his blue eyes.

"That's right, my father was a Scot," he explained. "And mother was an Apache, but I'm an Ojibway all the same. Call me Grey Owl."

"My Indian name's Anahareo," said the girl, who was petite, dark-eyed, and full of life. "But my nickname's Pony."

"Anahareo," Grey Owl repeated. "You Indians have lovely names."

"Oh, it's 'you Indians', is it? I thought you were an Ojibway." She laughed, and Grey Owl caught his breath at how pretty she was. "You don't seem to know if you're red or white. Better make up your mind."

He laughed too, and then began teasing her with a deadpan humour, which meant he was interested. Anahareo was both irritated and pleased by his jokes, but as the summer passed, their conversations grew more serious. She worked at the same resort, and there was time during the long evenings for him to tell her his dream of striking north, where the game had not yet been depleted by trappers and where the tourist was still a rarity.

That dream came true sooner than he expected. That

fall he got into a fight with the railway agent at Biscotasing. It ended disastrously, with Grey Owl tearing up the man's telegraph equipment by the wires and flinging it out the window. He had to leave the Algoma area in a hurry now, and so he set out alone to find his unspoiled wilderness. By January of the following year he had found a spot in Quebec, put up a snug cabin, and written Anahareo a letter asking her to join him.

They were married in an Indian ceremony at Lac Simon, and then his new bride was initiated into the wandering life of a part-time fire ranger, trapper, and guide.

"Why don't we build a real cabin and settle down?" she asked once, mopping her brow after a day-long canoe trip. "I could decorate it myself, and make the furniture too."

"No thanks, if you want domestic life, you've got the wrong man," he said, with a grim, almost fierce set to his mouth. "I'd suffocate if I had to stay in one place for long, so don't even think about it."

When it came to that, Anahareo herself didn't like sitting still. In winter she would fidget in the cold, lonely cabin, and she began to accompany Grey Owl on his trapping expeditions. With this woman beside him in the woods, he was forced to look at his profession through someone else's eyes, and did not like what he saw. He knew she was appalled by the cruelty of the traps. Too often they came upon an animal not quite killed by the iron teeth, and Grey Owl would have to finish the job by hand. Sometimes the fox or mink would be frozen rigid in a twisted shape, or, worst of all, there would be only a bloody paw, gnawed off by the animal in its desperation to escape.

Once, a mangled lynx slipped from Grey Owl's grasp before he could administer the death stroke. Instead of heading for the undergrowth, it dragged itself to Anahareo's feet, its hideous cries ringing through the woods like those of a wounded child. Grey Owl's axe soon put an end to its misery, but there was nothing he could do to lessen the misery in Anahareo's eyes. She said nothing, but he knew how much she hated the work. Sometimes, finding a rabbit or a weasel in the traps, he would think of his menagerie in the attic at Hastings. How tenderly he had cared for his animals then, the brothers of the ones he was now destroying.

Prices for fur were low that year, and his earnings for the winter were poor. Reluctantly, he planned a spring hunt. No trapper likes to do this, since so many of the newborn animals are killed along with the others. But he needed the money, and there would be no tourists this far north to give him work as a guide during the summer.

One evening, Grey Owl scooped up a trap from the lake and found to his horror that it contained the tiny, drowned bodies of three beaver kittens. He looked guiltily towards the beaver lodge for the mother, but there was no sign of her. When he returned to the cabin, he told Anahareo what had happened.

"You must stop this work," she said with sudden intensity. "It is killing your spirit as well as mine."

"I know that," he said, hanging his head. "But how else can we live?"

The next day they both canoed back to the beaver

lodge, where Grey Owl spotted what looked like a small muskrat. He stood up in the canoe and aimed his rifle at it, when another little animal popped up directly in the line of fire.

"More beaver kittens," he said.

"We must save them," Anahareo said at once.

"All right, we'll take them home," Grey Owl said, not realizing that with these words he had reached a turning point in his life.

The two beavers, christened McGinnis and McGinty, were affectionate bundles of fur who soon accepted the humans as their rightful parents. They were fed with a twig dipped in condensed milk, and Anahareo arranged a sleeping box filled with moss and leaves. The two Macs wrestled with each other, carried firewood all over the cabin, explored, whined, chattered, and in general, carried on like active, contented children. They only cried when Anahareo was out of sight, so she began sleeping on the floor to keep them happy.

"They're great pets, aren't they?" she said, cuddling one in her arms as it gently nibbled her finger.

"Pets, nothing!" Grey Owl said. "We're going to sell them as soon as I can get into town. There's a good price for live beaver, and trapping this year has been terrible."

Anahareo's heart almost broke at this news, but she realized that it was no use arguing when Grey Owl had his mind set on something. Since he was away in the bush all day, he hadn't seen enough of McGinnis and McGinty to fall under their bright-eyed spell.

On the trip into town the beavers were put into a small, metal stove, but they made such a racket that Grey Owl stopped early for the night to figure out a better sort of pen. After a swim and a meal, McGinnis went over to Grey Owl and began combing himself with the special claw beavers use for grooming. Then he investigated Grey Owl's face, nuzzled under his chin, and after several satisfied beaver noises, curled up and went to sleep on his chest.

Anahareo noticed the look of delight on her husband's face and began to feel a little better. Maybe all was not lost.

After a few days they reached the outskirts of town. Grey Owl took Anahareo aside and said: "You must think I'm a monster, but I didn't know that the beavers were...like that."

"You mean you won't sell them?"

"Not a chance of it!"

Alone on his fire-ranger's tower during the summer, Grey Owl had time to do some hard thinking. He had always been uneasy about the way beaver were hunted in the bush, and the arrival of the two Macs into his life brought the problem closer to home. Beaver had once been abundant in Europe and the United States, where they were now relatively scarce. In Canada, a whole nation had been built on beaver furs, but no one seemed to care that the animal was being wiped out. There was open season on beaver in most provinces, and as a trapper, Grey Owl knew how easily the few laws regarding their preservation could be evaded. Something had to be done.

"I'm off the beaver hunt for good," he told Anahareo during the last week of his ranger job.

"That suits me fine," she said enthusiastically. "But what will you do instead?"

"I am now the President, Treasurer and sole member

of the Society of the Beaver People. How about a donation?"

His plan was to find a remote lake with a good beaver population and to start a full-scale colony for conserving them. The area would have to be rich in other fur-bearing animals as well, for he still needed to trap to support himself. After he heard glowing reports about the Lake Temiscouata region on the Quebec-New Brunswick border, he and his "family" set out to try the experiment.

Everything about their arrival in Cabano, the town nearest Temiscouata, seemed to promise good times ahead. At the station, McGinnis and McGinty whined pathetically in their stove, and word got around that this Indian couple had an odd kind of papoose-board for their babies. The townspeople crowded to the station with gifts and food — hoping to catch a glimpse of the children. When Grey Owl showed them the beavers instead, they were delighted. So was Grey Owl, when the local storekeeper gave him full winter supplies on credit. At that time, he and Anahareo had less than fifty cents between them.

But if the people were nice, the country around Lake Temiscouata was a great disappointment. It had been logged and hunted over many times, and the animal population was low. To make matters worse, the two Macs caught a disease which made their fur fall out in handfuls. They looked like shrivelled, little, old men without their glorious coats, and grew depressed, whimpering to their humans to make it all grow back again.

Grey Owl decided to press farther north. After a

rough pack-trip in the biting snows of early winter, they reached Birch Lake and built a cabin. There were enough supplies for the season, but Grey Owl was worried. He had seen few signs of the animals he would have to trap to make the winter pay. By good luck, however, there was a live beaver house in the lake, with at least six inhabitants. McGinnis and McGinty greeted their new surroundings with squeals of joy and soon their fur had all grown in again.

But Grey Owl had to face the truth: there was no reason to go trapping in this area unless he broke his vow about killing beaver, and he could not bring himself to do that. To keep himself busy, he began to write down some of his stories of the wilderness, which Anahareo encouraged him to develop into a article. He sent the completed effort to *Country Life*, a British magazine for wealthy landowners who led a very different kind of country life than he did.

A bright spot in this gloomy winter was the Christmas celebration, which included toys for the two Macs, and a tree hung with chocolate, nuts, pitted prunes and other beaver delicacies. But much of the time Grey Owl brooded about getting a job at a sawmill, since he certainly couldn't support a wife and a beaver colony on the fifteen dollars a month from his war pension check.

In March, a heftier check was waiting in the post office. It was from *Country Life*, for his article, and with it came the suggestion that the editors would be interested in a book-length work from the new author.

Jubilant, Grey Owl and Anahareo returned to the cabin, where they found Dave, an old trapper friend, waiting to greet them. He laughed at the tricks of the two Macs, and then, grinning from ear to ear, presented Grey Owl with a gift.

"Thought I might as well make myself useful while you was away," he said shyly. "It might help out on your money troubles too. Is...is anything wrong?"

Grey Owl and Anahareo looked at each other in despair. The gift was a stack of beaver hides. Thinking to help, Dave had killed all the beaver in Birch Lake, thus putting to an end their plans for a colony. Feebly they tried to thank Dave, and then Anahareo burst into tears.

But worse was to come. With the breaking up of the ice, McGinnis and McGinty went out swimming one evening, never to return. They searched for weeks, Grey Owl limping because the soggy weather had made his sore foot swell to double its size, but there was no sign of the two Macs.

"I guess a trapper got to them," Grey Owl said despondently. "Some conservationists we turned out to be."

When Dave offered them two orphaned beaver kittens he had found by accident, Grey Owl wanted to refuse, but Anahareo spoke up: "All our losses just go to prove how much the beaver really do need protection. Giving up isn't going to help one bit."

They took the new kittens, but fate wasn't through with them yet, and the male died after a few weeks. However, the female seemed to thrive on human attention, and soon grew fat and rather bossy. Early on, she decided that she was going to be in charge of the household, and made her wishes clear with an imperious snarl or a wiggle of an increasingly large and gleaming behind. She fell madly in love with Grey Owl, and was always taking him by the trouser-leg and dragging him outside to see something she had built. They named her Jelly Roll.

Almost flat broke by now, Grey Owl decided to try for a guide's job at the resort town of Métis Beach. There was no work, however, and they spent several weeks near starvation — camping out near the resort hotel and wondering what to do. Jelly Roll grew frantic cooped up in her stove: she smelled the nearby Gulf of St Lawrence which drove her wild with the desire to go swimming, but she could not be allowed in salt water.

She lost weight, and Grey Owl was afraid she might start shedding her fur as well. In desperation, he set up a sign outside his tent: SEE THE BEAVER, 10¢. A few children came in, but their shrieks of laughter upset Jelly Roll. She snarled and reared up on her hind legs in rage, and this only made the children screech all the louder. Some were reaching out their sticky fingers to pat the soft coat when Grey Owl ushered them out of the tent and closed the exhibit.

Then a lady at the hotel heard about the problem and not only found Jelly Roll a fresh-water pond, but also arranged a lecture for Grey Owl, after reading some of his manuscripts. Grey Owl was terrified. How could he stand up in front of all those people? Who would want to hear anything he had to say? Surely his voice would crack, or his knees shake. As he wrote in his autobiography, *Pilgrims of the Wild*, when he faced the crowd he felt "like a snake that has swallowed an icicle, chilled from one end to the other."

But after it was over, he received loud applause. A British officer got up and said: "It is not a lecture you have given us tonight, my good man, but a poem about the wilderness."

They made enough money on lectures at Métis Beach to last another winter, although it was to be a lonely one for Grey Owl. Anahareo went north, thinking she would prospect for gold and set their financial worries at rest forever. Grey Owl intended to go, but at the last minute decided to stay near Birch Lake, on the chance that McGinnis and McGinty would return. He settled into a quiet period — writing his book, *The Vanishing Wilderness*, and watching Jelly Roll build her personal version of a beaver lodge, with the tunnel opening directly into the cabin floor. The spring brought Anahareo back, without gold, but happy to be home.

One evening when Grey Owl and Anahareo returned from a canoe trip, they found two white men waiting for them at the cabin. The older one rose to his feet and said: "I'm with the National Parks. Where's this beaver of yours?"

Surprised and a little apprehensive, Grey Owl motioned to the canoe, where Jelly Roll had lowered herself to the shore and was now toddling up to investigate the strangers.

The National Parks man stared for a moment, and then called to his assistant: "Quick Bill, let's shoot."

With lightning speed Anahareo swept up Jelly Roll into her arms and backed away. Grey Owl lunged at the man, but missed him. Then he turned, fumbling for his knife.

"Hey now, calm down," said the Parks man. "We just want to get a picture of her."

Feeling suddenly foolish, Grey Owl looked over at Bill, who was fiddling with a movie camera on a tripod.

"Put down the beaver," suggested the Parks man, "and let's talk this over."

Upset by all the commotion, Jelly Roll bustled around the camp — grunting and squeaking in indignation as the humans consulted. The Parks man was in charge of publicity, and he thought there might be a good film involving Jelly Roll which would advertise Canada's wilderness areas. He grew more friendly as he talked and soon was listening with interest to Grey Owl's idea of setting up a beaver sanctuary. His eyes really lit up when he heard about the *Country Life* article, the lectures in Métis Beach, and the book Grey Owl had written that winter.

"I think you and the National Parks Service should get together," he said. "But first let's see if Jelly Bean, or whatever her name is, is camera-shy."

There was no need to worry about that. From the moment the camera was trained on her, Jelly Roll proved that she was a natural ham. She sashayed around the cabin like an important movie star, doing her tricks and responding to direction with the flair of a professional.

It was not long after this that she had a companion. One morning, Grey Owl visited a trap he had set for an otter; instead, he found a male beaver caught by the leg. He took it home and did his best to repair the damaged foot, although there was little he could do about the large portion of scalp hanging from the animal's head. This piece of skin soon dried and Grey Owl was able to clip it off. This inspired the beaver's name: Rawhide.

Jelly Roll was in a frenzy of jealousy over the newcomer, and Grey Owl had to keep the door bolted to separate them. At last Rawhide was cured, and, with some regret, Grey Owl took the beaver out in the canoe and let him over the side on Jelly Roll's little gangplank. To Grey Owl's surprise, the beaver did not swim away, but followed the canoe. When Grey Owl extended his hand over the side, Rawhide came close and nuzzled it; when he let down the gangplank again, Rawhide scampered right up into the canoe. Grey Owl was amazed: he had tamed a wild beaver!

But there was no way that Rawhide and Jelly Roll would ever live in peace, so the male would have to go back to the lodge — forever, so Grey Owl thought. Then one day he returned to the camp to find Jelly Roll had been attacked by some animal, and by her side, licking her wounds, was Rawhide. Clearly Jelly Roll would have died if Rawhide had not defended her, and from that day on he was well established in the lady's favour. She was still the boss, but Rawhide was now a permanent fixture in the camp at Birch Lake.

They were not to stay there much longer, however. The National Parks man wrote: his film starring Jelly Roll, *The Beaver People*, had been well received, and the Government was now willing to pay all expenses if Grey Owl would set up a beaver sanctuary in Riding Mountain National Park, Manitoba. *Country Life* also announced that it was publishing the book: although when *The Vanishing Wilderness* appeared, Grey Owl was furious to find that the title had been changed to *The Men of the Last Frontier*, and that there had been many other changes made without his consent.

Riding Mountain was the wrong place for the sanctuary. There was a drought: the Manitoba sun shone without mercy and the lake shrank until it almost disappeared into the mud. Rawhide and Jelly Roll grew sickly and sluggish, and in desperation Grey Owl appealed to the Government for another location. The new site, in Prince Albert National Park, Saskatchewan, was just right, and on the shores of Lake Ajawaan Grey Owl began what was to become a prosperous beaver colony. The book was selling reasonably well, and to add to their happiness Anahareo gave birth to a daughter, Dawn, in August 1932.

The next year Grey Owl wrote his best-selling *Pilgrims of the Wild*, which included an autobiographical account of his experiences with beavers. In 1935, he also used McGinnis and McGinty — called Chilawee and Chikanee — in a story written for his daughter, Dawn, which became the well-known *Adventures of Sajo and her Beaver People*.

Across the muddy bottom of the empty pond the two big beavers struggled slowly, painfully and pitifully on their short and weary legs towards their unprotected home and babies, while within the lodge, huddled together, their tiny hands clutched tightly in each other's woolly fur, four helpless kitten beavers stared in terror at a sleek, black monster with a flat, evil head, that crept slowly through the entrance towards them, his teeth bared, hissing like a snake as he came. Negik, the Otter, the hungry, the cruel and the sly, having broken the dam and so drained the pond, could now get what he had come for — kitten beaver meat! Now was his time. His snaky body blocked the plunge-hole; there seemed to be no escape. He gathered his legs beneath him, ready to spring.

During the battle between the otter and the parent beavers, who return to the lodge in the nick of time, two of the kittens are lost. The story is about an Indian girl and her brother who raise the two beaver kittens, lose one of them, and are reunited with it after a series of adventures. It is Grey Owl's most delightful book, an added asset being his own pencil sketches used as illustrations.

Now in his mid-forties, and known throughout North America and Europe through films and books, Grey Owl nevertheless began to feel that his life had gone stale. There was really nothing for him to do at Lake Ajawaan; the beavers were looking after themselves very nicely, and money was no worry. Anahareo was growing bored and restless in their modern, well-furnished cabin — especially when he was writing and lost in another world which had no room for her.

She renewed her interest in mineralogy with a correspondence course, and took off on frequent prospecting trips — leaving Dawn with friends in Prince Albert. Grey Owl envied her the trips; it was lonely and dull with her away, and he longed to be out in the bush himself. But nothing seemed to have zest for him any more, and he still felt like a stranger in the western landscape. He missed the look of the Quebec and Ontario wilderness; he spent a lot of time dreaming about the old days and longing to see his former bush-mates.

In 1935, Lovat Dickson, his new English publisher, invited him across the Atlantic on a four-month tour, and the Canadian Government supported the scheme as good publicity. Grey Owl was reluctant, remembering his last visit to England during the war. What was the point of returning to a place that had never given him anything but pain and spiritual distress? And yet, what was the point of turning into a vegetable in Saskatchewan? Perhaps the trip would snap him out of his apathy, and at least he would be doing some good by promoting the cause of conservation.

At last he agreed to go, realizing how much money it would mean for Dawn when she grew up. As he had feared, the tour was a nightmare for him. He had lectured to small groups before, but the thought of facing huge London crowds paralysed him with stage fright. He felt uneasy in the city and spent much of his spare time pacing his room on silent, moccasined feet. "I feel like a man standing naked upon a rock," he told his friend and advisor Lovat Dickson.

Dickson hit on the scheme of camping out whenever possible in Epping Forest, a small woods on the outskirts of London. There, relaxing by an open fire, Grey Owl could refresh himself before going back into the strange, unfriendly world of the city. His lectures were a huge success: the English people, exhausted by World War I and weary of the Depression, were eager to hear this noble figure of a man clad in buckskin speak to them about the wonders of the faraway wilderness. Financially the tour was a triumph, but perhaps the price Grey Owl paid was too great. The picture of health when he arrived in England, he began to look tired and old as the tour continued.

Reporters and photographers followed his every step, and he answered their questions with an unhappy mixture of fear and hostility. Once a photographer asked him to pat a policeman's horse on the nose. "That's the kind of stuff our readers lap up," he said. "All the guck about animals."

Grey Owl drew himself to his full height and stared down at the photographer, who began fidgeting with his collar. He gripped the man by the arm and said in a quiet, intense way: "I think you've got me wrong, brother."

Then he turned to Dickson and said: "Let's get out of here." His face had the strained, hunted expression which was to become familiar to people who knew him during the last years of his life.

At last the tour was over. But when Grey Owl returned to Canada, he found he was a famous figure at home too, and the press and public gave him no peace. Hoping that the wilderness could heal his wounded spirit, he hurried back to Prince Albert. But something within him had changed. He walked around the lake and the beaver lodges like a dead man, unable to shake off his feelings of apathy and despair. He suffered from fainting fits at this time too, although the doctors could find nothing physically wrong. Naturally his condition upset Anahareo, who had spent a dreary time of it while he was away, and now grew uneasy in the cabin with a sick and troubled man. Finally it was decided that they should separate for good, Anahareo taking Dawn with her.

The life that Grey Owl had built now seemed to him more than ever a hopeless wreck. With a great effort of will, he roused himself to new projects — spending a lot of money to make a movie about northern Ontario in summer, and starting a new book, *Tales of the Empty Cabin*. There was a brief spell of sunshine in this bleak period when he met, and shortly afterwards married, Yvonne Perrier, a French-Canadian girl with Indian ancestry. But even this new love could not change the deep unhappiness he felt in his heart, and in 1937 he agreed to do another lecture tour of England, not much caring what happened to him any more.

As far as the public was concerned, this second tour was an even bigger hit than the first. He was presented to the King and Queen — giving a private lecture for them at Buckingham Palace. By now his speaking style was perfected: his deep, rich voice and dramatic presentation thrilled his listeners. But each performance seemed to drain more life from the man, and he went about from day to day like a machine wound up with a key. A spark of his former self flashed out, however, when the BBC asked him to speak on their Children's Hour, and then rejected his script because it condemned the cruelty of fox hunting. If he would simply take out the fox hunting reference, they said, there would be no problem.

Always quick to anger at changes made in his writing, Grey Owl stormed into Broadcasting House and confronted a junior executive, a chilly young woman with horn-rimmed glasses and hair done up in a bun.

"I'm terribly sorry," she said, "but our regulations forbid us saying anything derogatory about fox hunting. So many of our listeners hunt, don't you know."

"Then they should be aware of the pain and anguish it causes the fox," Grey Owl said with dangerous calm. "There is no sport in running a defenceless animal to earth."

"It's an easy enough matter to take out the offensive statement. Our regulations...."

"I'll take back my script, since it so offends you. I won't permit it to be used," Grey Owl snapped. "And you know what you can do with your regulations!"

"Well, sir, no need to be so huffy about such a little thing. After all, rules are rules."

Grey Owl glared in speechless fury at the woman, who only glared back with cold, stubborn eyes. The anger suddenly drained out of him. What was the use of wasting energy on this stupid white man's world with its timid little regulations anyway? Without another word, he turned and walked out. The talk was never broadcast, but in its printed version — with the fox-hunting reference left in — it sold a healthy ten thousand copies.

Back in North America, he was restless, giving many lectures in Canada and the United States before he returned to Saskatchewan. His new wife, Yvonne, had to go to hospital in Regina, so he went on to Prince Albert alone. Crossing the little Main Street to the National Parks Office, he saw something that brought him out of his listlessness with a jolt. Across the street, Anahareo and Dawn were walking hand in hand, smiling and chattering to each other in the soft March sunshine.

He lifted his hand to wave, but then drew it back. He had no right to see them now: he had another woman, and for all he knew, Anahareo might have remarried as well.

But it was too late. Dawn caught sight of him and ran towards him calling out "Daddy Grey Owl!" Anahareo followed Dawn across the street, her smile changing slightly when she saw how thin and worn his face had become. They talked in friendly, general terms about the future, then shook hands and went on their separate ways. Outwardly it looked like a mere chance encounter between old friends, but somewhere within himself Grey Owl knew it was his last meeting with the woman who had been the great love of his life.

He went alone to Lake Ajawaan, where it was still deep winter. He made no attempt to look for Jelly Roll and Rawhide, who were somewhere in a cosy beaver lodge, locked in by the frozen surface of the lake. As he tramped along the ice-crusted shoreline, the wind cutting through his chest like a knife, he thought that at least he had done this one good thing in his life: he had provided a sanctuary for his "beaver people". As for the rest — the fame, the public appearances, the money — it meant nothing.

Suddenly he felt dizzy, and a sharp, burning sensation spread through his lungs. He turned on unsteady legs; it was a long way back to the cabin.

Several hours later the telephone rang at a nearby ranger station. The person who answered heard only the following words: "Come quickly....I am ill...."

Grey Owl was taken to the hospital in Prince Albert by a horse-drawn sleigh. The diagnosis was pneumonia, with temperatures well above the hundred mark. On April 13, 1938, Grey Owl — sometimes called Wa-Sha-

Quon-Asin or Archie Belaney — died. A day later, the press began its accusations.

The hubbub that followed his death seems stupid and unfair today. Newspaper writers had tried to turn him into a spotless hero, and had labelled him — to his enormous disgust — a "modern Hiawatha" and a "St Francis of the Indians". When they found he was no angel they tried to make him a devil, and dredged up every doubtful aspect of his life, from his drinking bouts to his four wives. But they were most upset by his whiteness. Grey Owl's adoption by the Ojibways, his wide knowledge of Indian customs and language, the defence of the red man's rights in his books, his own style of life — none of it seemed to make any difference to a society that felt it had been fooled.

A minority reminded people of the man's contributions to conservation and literature. What difference did race make, when he had done so much for the world? Few cared to see this point of view. Perhaps deep down, people were disturbed by the thought that a white man would actually prefer a more primitive culture to his own "advanced" society. In this, Grey Owl was like another controversial Englishman of the time, Lawrence of Arabia, who also seemed to lose his lust for life when he returned to his own civilization.

For truly, in his last years Grey Owl seemed like a man waiting to die, and no doctor could understand what caused his terrible depressions. Perhaps the pressures of fame were just too much for a solitary man of the woods to handle. The breakdown in his relationship with Anahareo was certainly a factor, as was the feeling that he had already achieved his goal, that there was nothing left to live for. Perhaps in his heart he felt the heavy strain of being accepted as an Indian by all the world, when he knew that by birth he was not.

Possibly he did not know. His mother's fantastic stories about his father may have included some details to make him think that he did have Indian blood. It is not hard to imagine that his childhood fantasy might have turned an English mother, Katherine Cox, into the Apache princess, Katherine Cochise. And if the public would only listen to his message about the vanishing wilderness and the extinction of the beaver from the lips of a *full*-blooded Indian, it was worth a bit of play-acting to get that message across.

There are many unanswered questions about this strange man, but we can be sure that he was not deliberately deceiving the public for his own personal gain. His earnings often went straight into conservation projects for the northern wilds he described so eloquently in his books. And if ever a white man had earned the right to speak for the Indian, the wilderness, and the beaver, that man was Grey Owl.

# notes

The best source for information about Ernest Thompson Seton is his autobiography, *Trail of an Artist-Naturalist* (New York: Scribner's, 1940), written when the author was eighty. There is also a short biography by W. and S. Garst: *Ernest Thompson Seton* (New York: Messner, 1959). *Wild Animals I Have Known* is now in paperback, with the author's own drawings (New York: Schocken SB 139, 1966).

Elsie M. Pomeroy's *Sir Charles G. D. Roberts* (Toronto: Ryerson, 1943) is the standard biography. There is a good brief treatment of the life in W. J. Keith's *Charles G. D. Roberts* (Toronto: Copp Clark, 1969). A paperback anthology of Roberts' best nature stories has been edited by Alec Lucas: *The Last Barrier and Other Stories* (Toronto: McClelland & Stewart, 1958).

Most of Grey Owl's books are autobiographical, especially *Pilgrims of the Wild*. The best all-round biography is Lovat Dickson's *Half-Breed* (London: Peter Davies, 1939). Anahareo's *Devil in Deerskins* (Toronto: new press, 1972) is an interesting account, adding new information. Donald B. Smith's article "Grey Owl", in *Ontario History* for September 1971, is brief, accurate, and worthwhile. All of Grey Owl's books are available from Macmillan of Canada — four of the five in paperback.

The author is indebted to the above sources, and wishes also to thank the following individuals for their help: Dee Barber, Kent Bush, Jay Macpherson, Lady Roberts, Donald B. Smith, John Wadland, and Albert Wilson for the Estate of Sir Charles G. D. Roberts.

Both author and publishers wish to acknowledge the following sources for illustrations and quoted materials: Henry E. Huntingdon Library, San Marino, California (page 10); *Codex Canadensis*, Thomas Gilcrease Institute, Tulsa, Oklahoma (page 13 top); John Wadland (pages 16, 39); E. T. Seton, *Two Little Savages*, copyright 1959 by Grace Gallatin Seton, Doubleday (pages 26-7); Art Gallery of Ontario (page 40 top); Seton Memorial Library and Museum, Philmont Scout Ranch, Cimmaron, New Mexico (pages 40 bottom, 41); Seton, *Trail of an Artist-Naturalist* (page 53); Ontario Archives (pages 62, 123-4, 125 top); Douglas Library, Queen's University, Kingston, Ontario (page 78 bot.); *The New York Evening Journal*, copyright 1907 by *American-Journal-Examiner* (page 78 bottom); Roberts, *Red Fox*, Farrar, Straus and Giroux, photograph by the Metropolitan Library Board (pages 78-9); Roberts, *The Feet of the Furtive*, Ryerson, photograph by the Metropolitan Library Board

## notes

(page 79); *Selected Poems of Sir Charles G. D. Roberts* (page 81); Roberts, *Thirteen Bears*, Ryerson (page 92); National and Historic Parks Branch, Department of Indian Affairs and Northern Development (page 100); and Information Canada Photothèque (page 125 top); Grey Owl, *The Adventures of Sajo and her Beaver People,* Macmillan of Canada (page 139).